AF255224

Story Theology

Story Theology

Exploring Themes of the Gospel through Stories

J. A. KAYS

RESOURCE *Publications* · Eugene, Oregon

STORY THEOLOGY
Exploring Themes of the Gospel through Stories

Resource Publications
An Imprint of Wipf and Stock Publishers
199 W. 8th Ave., Suite 3
Eugene, OR 97401

www.wipfandstock.com

PAPERBACK ISBN: 978-1-6667-3892-6
HARDCOVER ISBN: 978-1-6667-3893-3
EBOOK ISBN: 978-1-6667-3894-0

02/06/23

To Tara. You are the best thing.

"To be stories at all they must be a series of events:
but it must be understood that this series—the plot,
as we call it—is only really a net whereby to catch
something else."

—C. S. Lewis,
On Stories: And Other Essays on Literature

Contents

Acknowledgments

I am deeply indebted to Richard Lischer for all his guidance, grace, and encouragement through this writing project. His wisdom and that of Sarah Musser helped me to formulate a DMin thesis that transformed into this work.

A. Joseph Everson's influence, mentoring, and friendship early in my college years through today have shaped my entire life trajectory.

Thank you to Duke Divinity School and Will Willimon, who is always liable to ridicule my Southern California ways. To my Duke cohort, your comedic relief, acceptance of me, and love for God are unmatched.

Journey the Church—you are my people and have always loved and supported me.

Thank you to my mom, who bought me Harry Potter books, and my dad, who made me memorize Robert Frost.

To Tara, my wife and best friend, there are no words worthy of your sacrifice and love for me.

And Zeke, Etta, and Norah—none of you can read yet, but thanks for your patience and every reminder for me not to take myself so seriously.

Introduction

We understand who we are and the world we live in only because of story. Without story, it is impossible to define our identity, meaning, purpose, or action. The Bible, after all, is a story—it begins with Alpha and ends with Omega. It is God's story—the story of everything. By it, we learn how the Christian story is not a piece of a larger story but claims to be *the* story in which other stories find their place.

To answer the biggest questions about who we are and the world we live in, we must use a story. So, this book uses just that—story to communicate theological truth. I explore ten central themes of the Gospel (*Hesed* "steadfast love," *Hamartia* "sin," *Pistis* "faith," *Qadosh* "holy," *Chara* "joy," *Tov* "good," *Elpis* "hope," *Splagchnizomai* "compassion," *Aphiemi* "forgiveness," and *Shalom* "peace") through short stories.

At the end, there's a notes section for each chapter where I provide theological research and analysis for each story. It's a bit like spilling the beans, but the careful analysis should give new insights into each theme of the gospel I explore.

In creating this collection, I hope to provide a unique resource for theological reflection that's helpful for anybody who's willing to step into a story.

—J. A. Kays

1

Hesed

SHE FINALLY FINDS THE remote wedged between old cups of coffee and rust-colored pill bottles. The pills rattle in their tubes like snakes in the grass. Leftover coffee slinks to the other side of the ceramic as she takes hold of the remote. Her thumb on the power button sends the room to near blackness, and the gargle of the news anchor silences. The shifting glow on the wall darkens. The reflection of happy family photos of days gone by turns black.

A streetlamp cuts through the blinds to illuminate bills, magazines, and final notices leaning like the Tower of Pisa. The tabby cat at her heels gives a soft purr and nuzzles against her woolen pants. She takes her coat and mittens, the house keys off the rack beside the door. And last, she grabs her purse and the world within it—what mothers grab to go anywhere.

With a switch of the deadbolt, she's greeted by a Minnesota chill that hits the nose, the throat, the lungs, and finally, the bones. She crosses the threshold and steps out into the crunch of snow.

"Geez, Louise, it's gonna be a cold one! A polar vortex coming down on the Twin Cities . . . like the Halloween blizzard of '91!"

It's what the weatherman said.

The stroll to the bus stop today's a trek. It feels like Everest or any of those tall peaks they show on Discovery.

One boot in front of the other. It's what she tells herself.

She stops at the corner of Monroe and Second Ave. There's an alcove where the door opens to the brick building—Olson's Butcher. And there, in the light of the butcher's shop and sheltered from the storm, she checks her watch. The watch with the red robins on a branch tells her it's 4:26am Saturday, January 14th.

She still has two blocks to trudge, and at her *one boot in front of the other* pace, it's cutting rather close. She readjusts her coat, buttons, zips straight to the throat, and sets out again into the blur.

One boot in front of the other.

It's not so tough now, with only one block to go. The wind howls, and the January snow speeds horizontally, like someone's shredding carpet up ahead.

Half a block to go.

But there, swinging around the corner of Second Ave and Mt. Zion, low-beam headlights scan across the streets of tundra. She quickens her pace, as fast as her late sixties can handle. Her blood pressure meds kick in overtime.

Tommy wouldn't leave without me, right? she worries.

No, yeah, he'll wait, I'm sure of it.

Her conclusion proves true. The bus idles, waiting for no one—except for the snow and wind and a mother scampering in the dark. The hydraulics hiss as the door opens an oven in the middle of the arctic. She collapses into the rubber stairwell—heart racing, lungs pumping. But in no way does it keep her from her niceties—

"Tommy! It sure is a-coming down out there! How's your Ma doing?"

"Oh, she's all right, Ms. Nelson, she's just fine," Tommy says in a nasally voice.

Ms. Nelson shifts her purse and straightens her hat. She stomps the snow off her boots and climbs the final steps into the belly of the bus. Four rows back and to the right, she takes her usual seat. The cushions are ratty, but they form to her figure. It's only every Saturday she rides the bus, but the creases and tears in her seat are now something of a comfort to her.

Her heart still thumps in her chest, her lungs thawing. With her head pressed against the glass, a circle of fog expands with each breath. She closes her eyes. In the gentle rumble of the diesel, her heart rate slows, and her lungs ease. Tommy shifts into gear. Her body moves with the way of the bus. And the tires crawl forward.

"Kreeeeek!" The bus lurches ahead and swings sharply back.

"Uh . . . Ms. Nelson, we're here!" Tommy calls from behind the wheel.

She shakes off the slumber and opens her eyes to a white wasteland. There's nothing but blue and white to the west. To her right sits a dull town whose buildings look draped in paper mâché.

She stands to her feet with a heavy sigh and walks forward. She thanks Tommy for the ride and exits into the cold. It's not so bad now that the sun's up and the wind's down. It's a bit of mercy, she supposes. A lot can change in three hours. Time has a way of doing that.

She peels back her sleeve, exposing her wrist to the chill—the robins say it's 7:32am. There's no time change across the state line— no going back.

The truth is, Tommy had made good time, even with a snow-storm—maybe too good of time. She still has twenty-eight minutes until they open the cages. It's not enough time to step into Swenson's Diner for a cup 'o joe and a blueberry muffin, but surely enough to walk six blocks and the long, lonely stretch before the prison.

One boot in front of the other.

That's it.

One boot in front of the other.

Three blocks to go.

One boot in front—It's colder than it looks with the clear skies.

Two blocks.

One.

And there, a long, lonely stretch away, stands a giant mon-strosity. The sharp edges and cold walls sprout from the snow, me-tallic and stone.

Maximum Security Prison, the signpost reads.

Another placard stands out like a school bus against the snow—

Hitchhikers may be escaping inmates.

Not her boy, though. They keep death row locked down. Well, at least since 1984, when the Virginia 6 made a break for it. On one of those true crime shows, she heard they made it to North Carolina—Philadelphia—as far as Vermont—five miles from the border. But it was short-lived. Within twelve years, all five were put out by the electric chair and the last by lethal injection.

But she doesn't concern herself with these things.

I'm here to see my boy. That's what she thinks.

One boot in front of the other.

The long, lonely stretch is a reverie of sorts, a playback of scenes over the years:

A bath in the kitchen sink. Crawling across the fraying linoleum. Peaches from the can on a hot summer night. Second-round elimination in the spelling bee. A broken wrist, a busted mailbox, the warped frame of the bike he got for Christmas. Prom Night in a rental tuxedo.

One boot in front of the other.

Two missing teeth and blood all over the sink—finally out after three days of dangling by a thread. Saturday morning cartoons. Times tables and struggling with long division.

One boot in front of the other.

A hit-by-a-pitch black eye. Putting Shadow down and crying at the vet. Punk rock music and learning the guitar.

One boot in front of the other.

It doesn't get any easier, even though it happens every Saturday—sun, rain, sleet, or snow. But it happens every Saturday.

And every Saturday, they look like crows, high up on the walls, perched in their towers, armed to the teeth with live ammunition. With their cold steel semi-automatic necklaces dangling, they look down. She looks up through the chain links topped with barbed wire bushes, and, unbelievably, she waves.

This is a Maximum Security Facility.

All visitors and their possessions are subject to search.

The arrow beside the letters V-I-S-I-T-A-T-I-O-N points toward a nondescript building. It's a world altogether unlike the free.

Fluorescent lights divide the room—from east to west, illuminating a cold, sterile waiting room. The plastic, hardback chairs line the square—bolted to the floor as if someone might walk off with such commodities for Craigslist. Or maybe it's a safety issue? The bulletproof glass separating loved ones from the law would surely withstand a chair flung at the force of human passion. But how might the nose, wrist, or ribcage of a loved one in the waiting room hold up? Not so good. Better bolt it down just to be safe.

She steps up to the counter like she's ordering lunch, just like they used to at Lucky's. It's the same as any grease joint where the saturated fats all taste the same, and there's a slimy pinball machine chirping in the back. But it was their special place. She'd make him order for himself, like a big boy, before he rushed off to slap the grimy buttons and try to keep the ball in play. Thanks to a quarter found in the cushions, he would be stimulated by the euphoria of lights and sound.

"Cheeseburger and fries!" he'd blurt out.

"And what do you say?" she'd correct him.

"Uh . . . Please!"

Marsha, behind the register, would smile, the gold caps on her molars shining.

"Sure, honey."

With his stubby fingers on the greasy counter, he'd push for more—striving to feed the insatiable craving of a five-year-old. He'd look back, doe-eyed, and ask:

"Mommy, can I get a strawberry shake too? Please, please, please?!"

She taps the three-quarter-inch glass, and the deputy looks up from the desktop computer. His expression is featureless—a by-the-book poker face—until his brain registers the familiar face before him. The sides of his mouth creep northward into a toothy grin. The staunch, lawlike facade drops. It softens to resemble the polite, doe-eyed boy at Lucky's.

"Well, good mornin', Ms. Nelson," he says softly through the intercom.

His voice sounds fuzzy and small, but his smile never fades, and neither does his warmth as she slides her credentials through the stainless-steel tray. His fingers claw up on his end, catching her Minnesota I.D. between his nails and fingertips. Without even looking, though, he scribbles her information into the visitation logbook. Memorized. By heart.

"It's not often I see you here on Saturdays, Micah," she says.

"No, yeah, you're right. Sammy needed the shift covered. Kid's got the flu or something. Taking 'em all down. Every one of 'em like the plague."

"Oh, no. Heavens!"

"Yeah, MaryAnne's bringing over hotdish this evening, just dropping it on the doorstep. Suppose she better ring the bell; else it'll end up froze."

"Oh, Micah, you two are some pair."

"You betcha, Ms. Nelson. I'm a lucky man."

He finishes his scribbles in the logbook and slides her I.D. back across the bulletproof divide.

"Thanks," she smiles warmly.

But then, as she stares back, her smile drops and sags. Her expression returns to her reason for being here. It's not a grocery store encounter or catching up in the pews. She lets out a sigh that seems to say, *Well, here we are. Let's make the best of it.* But all the while, her eyes still stare. What is it, hope in there? Confidence? Resolve? The deputy just nods and turns his eyes away, unsure.

She turns from the glass, the greasy counter, Marsha, and memories of pinball bliss and slides onto an immovable chair.

This is a tobacco-free facility

State-approved I.D. only

No inappropriate clothing may be worn.

She has them memorized by heart.

All persons subject to search at all times

Visits may be monitored and/or recorded.

Every word, memorized.

Children must be kept under control at all times, or your visit may be terminated.

That's the one that always gets her.

She leans her head back and sees the full line of an artless room. She sees bare, painted walls—faded to eggnog. Surely no one chose this color in the first place. How long does it take for paint to turn? To lose its luster? As long as skin takes to wrinkle? Certainly, alabaster hasn't turned all the way to eggnog in the years she's been here, but maybe it's turned a shade or two.

Who picks the paint swatches for prisons anyways? It's probably a color without a name, like XE6642. It's what they do in here anyway, isn't it? Inmate number 06267–045. No names, just numbers erasing identity.

When her son was in high school, they spent a week picking the wallpaper off like scabs. They had three colors picked out and were armed with four rollers, two trays, and one drop cloth. After sampling each color, they went with the unanimous winner: 5007–7A semigloss.

Dressed in old, ratty clothes hardly distinguishable from their typical, everyday attire, they poured a can of 5007–7A into a tray. It's called Mystic Sea, but it's really seafoam, at least when it dried— the color of the sea and the sky. But for them, that day, it could've been any color. Who knows if any paint even got on the walls? It was a day the boy became a man, or at least a little older than a boy, or a more capable boy.

He moved the roller from the floor to the ceiling, running streaks like melted candle wax down the walls. It takes time to figure out the technique—motion, weight, and paint on the roller. They tried the "W's" and "M's" like Mike, the hardware store owner, showed them. But now, the streaks ran diagonally. What did they care? It's art, after all, the canvas of their home. It was a Saturday together with laughter and specks of paint like lice in the hair. It was such a momen—

—"BZZZZ!"

It sounds like a hammer electrified. The door opens. The deputy steps through, his boots clunking on the slick floors.

"Okay, folks, single-file line. Remember, no food, beverages, or smoking inside the visiting area. No cell phones, cameras, or weapons of any kind. Refusal to comply may result in your visit being denied or terminated."

The loved ones of those locked up line up, single file, like in kindergarten. They all hold the same look in their eyes. It's a look she used to wear—one that spoke and said—"I'd rather be anywhere but here." But the years had turned things over. For her, now, she'd rather be here than anywhere.

Electric hammer drops. They buzz through a door down a soulless corridor and come upon an elevator.

One boot in front of the other.

Eighteen steps to the door, three more forward, and four to the right.

Memorized. By heart.

She could do the walk in her sleep, as she often does.

Electric hammer drops. The door down the corridor locks.

It used to be that he'd carry his hammer everywhere—the plastic one that didn't leave dents in the drywall. He always wanted to be a worker man. That's what he called it since he was three.

He tried construction for a short while—said he was built for the job site, not the cubicle. He found fulfillment in pouring concrete, not college courses. Swinging a twenty-two-ounce hammer and driving nails left him more accomplished than Psych 202. How the sky could've been the limit had he stayed.

The loved ones crowd in, and the deputy presses level three. Pulleys and cables lift the metal box through concrete walls. They feel the floor surge upwards.

He had pressed every button—fifteen through G. It lit up like a Christmas tree—to the irritation of the other travelers. They braced for stops on every floor. The grin on his six-year-old face showed a sign of achievement—look what I accomplished.

Rosy with embarrassment, she apologized for his actions, hoping to defuse their anger. She even shaped her body to match the apology—shrugging her shoulders, exhaling a sigh of frustration, a slow shake of the head—as if to say—"I can't believe what's gotten into him!"

But she bit her lip to keep a smile from escaping. Deep down, she concealed the humor of it all. Just look at this—all these important suits slowed down from their deadlines and quarterly figures by a first grader pushing buttons. And once they're pressed, there's no un-pressing it.

The floor jumps at level three, and the doors split open. The line of fluorescents hum like gathering bees above, hovering down the hallway. Loved ones spill out into another soulless corridor with the same ugly paint job.

Sixteen steps forward.

She could do it blindfolded. Newcomers find it's a windowless maze—a complete loss of all sense of direction. But she knew every scuff in the flooring, every scratch along the wall.

They reach another door. Electric hammer drops. Then single file, the loved ones step into the room. Their hearts feel heavier than the usual ten or so ounces. Their lungs are filtered, like breathing through a cloth. Their eyes are unsure, scanning. It all produces an almost tangible substance that hangs in the air—grief, sorrow, expectation, hope, confusion, devotion, love.

Payphones stretch the length of the hallway, with each booth separated by too short of partitions. There's no privacy in prison. The thick, soundless glass reveals a mirror image of the other world: a payphone and an empty plastic chair.

She takes her seat at the next booth in sequence and waits. Her eyes dart and search. The phone before her is caked with the fingerprints of a previous loved one. The glass is smudged with palm streaks. As she looks out, through the glass, into a world altogether different from her own, she feels the thumping in her chest.

Her pulse still leaps—every Saturday. She looks down and glances at the robins—it's a quarter past eight. She sits and waits like she's waited all the time before.

It's just a stage, she told herself. It's the first trimester full of morning sickness, hormones, and mood swings. She was waiting for her body to become a home for him. At eight weeks, he was a kidney bean, then a kumquat, a lime, and later—a honeydew, a pineapple. And then, after a thirty-nine-week watermelon, he came. New. Brand new. Five pounds, fourteen ounces—a wait ever so worth it.

Electric hammer drops. An orange line shuffles in. Her heart runs, flushing blood throughout her body.

There he is—a five-pound, fourteen-ounce, thirty-nine-week watermelon. But somehow, he's different. He's years and ages and experiences different. And yet somehow, he's still the same.

The fluorescents highlight the sagging lids and dark circles beneath his eyes. His one hour of vitamin D a day, five days a week, is sorely deficient. Good luck finding a solid hour of sunlight any given week at this latitude—especially with all the snow and overcast.

He steps forward in line, swimming in an oversized smock.

Outside of this place, he could pass for anybody—a chef, a priest, a janitor, a baseball coach—he doesn't have the hardened look of a criminal. But what is that look? And how does he not have it?

The reality is, he's here. And she knows it all too well. And that's why she's here. Every Saturday. Sun, rain, sleet, or snow. It burns in her heart that this is where she comes to visit her son. Grief and anguish have racked her mind and body since he was taken away in the back of a police cruiser. *Why? Why? Why?* The questions suffocate. But it pales in compared to how the other family must feel. At least she can still visit her son. And despite the mixture of emotions, nothing stops her. Her life orders around it, shaped and molded to the necessity of Saturdays.

The robins say it's 8:17am. He shuffles up with a sheepish grin and sits in a plastic chair. He reaches up, and with both hands cuffed, he grabs the phone. He pulls the receiver to his ear and says:

"Hi, mom."

"Hiyah, sweetheart."

"Thanks for coming," he says, one hand around the phone, the other fumbling with its metal cord.

"You betcha. Wouldn't miss our Saturday for the world."

She dabs her eyes. He stares at his feet clasped at the ankles.

"So," she clears her throat, "what's new? You get a chance to read that book I told you about?"

"Yeah, Ma, all I got is time. It was a short read, anyway. The library had a copy. A hundred and twenty pages or something."

"You like it?" she asks.

"Sure," he replies.

"What's your take on it then?" she questions.

"Oh, I dunno," he mumbles.

"C'mon!" she nudges.

"Uh . . . well . . . I guess it's, uh, about not giving up."

"Uh-huh . . ." she encourages.

He continues, catching his stride, coming to life,

"But to have the catch of your life devoured by sharks? Now that's depressing. He should've had a bigger boat—like Jaws, remember? And some better gear, at least. I mean, come on!"

She nods and smiles, soaking in all the warmth of Cuban beaches and Caribbean air.

"And another thing is," he says, "a fisherman like Santiago who can't catch a fish for eighty-four days is probably in the wrong business."

They laugh and smile—exercising out-of-shape muscles.

Electric hammer drops. The deputy stands in the doorway.

Oh, but they've just begun! She checks the robins. *There must be some mistake!*

But the birds on the branch say it's 8:45am. She feels robbed by two minutes. One hundred and twenty seconds to hear from her boy. One hundred and twenty seconds to tell him all the things of love and care and support she could cram into one hundred and twenty ticks. *What happened to the time?*

He says, "Bye, mom."

"I love you, sweetheart."

"Love you too, mom."

He gently hangs the phone on the cradle hook. And with a slight smile, he returns to the line. A moment later, they hobble back to the cages. The gathering tears blur her eyes. She sees an orange haze, fading like the sunset, then gone.

Her tears never fail to run every Saturday. And a runny nose isn't far behind. She's long since given up on mascara.

It takes a moment until she realizes she's still clutching the phone, listening to silence, hoping for more. She sets the phone back in its place, adding her own fingerprints and residue for the next loved one to find. Then with a heavy sigh and a wipe across her face, she finds her feet.

One boot in front of the other.

God knows it's a mountain to climb, and she's spent. Exhausted. Not empty, but exhausted.

Electric hammers drop. Left and right, they crash, resounding as the line of loved ones maneuvers backward through the maze. Her breath is shallow and labored as she heads for escape. Her chest heaves and her lungs burn.

Sixteen steps forward.

The elevator plunges but at a belaboring rate. There's more buzzing, more doors to unlock and lock.

Four steps to the left, three more forward, and eighteen steps to the door.

How can you even breathe?

And there, where the signs tell the tale—*This is a tobacco-free facility,* and *Children must be kept under control at all times, or your visit may be terminated*—it's almost to where she can. But here, in the lackluster room, she doesn't dare forgo her niceties:

"Thank you, Micah," she smiles at the deputy.

"'til next week, Ms. Nelson?"

"You betcha. Please give my love to Sammy and his family. Oh, and also, to your sweetheart of a wife."

She walks out, and the winter air fills her lungs. It's reviving, almost awakening.

She pauses to catch her breath and wipe away the tears before they freeze. Then she sets out across the long, lonely stretch away from her son's home.

One boot in front of the other.

She treks six blocks and pops into Swenson's Diner for a cup 'o joe, a blueberry muffin, or maybe a piece of cherry pie. He always liked banana cream, but she needs something extra sweet and warm today.

She checks the robins: 10:17am. It's eighteen minutes until Tommy turns home. She wraps her fingers around the mug, savoring the last bit of warmth from the refill. The check says $4.75. She leaves it on the table with a three-and-a-half-dollar tip. It's a few bills, but mostly coins.

All bundled up, she steps out into the polar vortex and makes her way to the greyhound.

Tommy rumbles through the white across a dark stretch of road. Four rows back and to the right, her eyes catch all the frozen tundra they previously missed. For three hours, she stares out. Her mind wanders from a thirteen by seven-foot cell to a rental tuxedo to a bare oak tree by a barn to the east.

The tires slow up into town, gliding across the snowy roads and slowing to a stop. As with every Saturday, she thanks Tommy for the safe trip.

"See you next week, Ms. Nelson?"

"You betcha, Tommy."

She descends the rubber stairwell and out into the cold.

2

Hamartia

THE ALUMINUM CANS CLATTER with a tin empty tune. They shiver together, bounced by each bump in the road. Unfinished drops of barley and yeast seep out onto the carpeted floorboard. The liquid coagulates with the days of spent cigarettes and fast-food wrappers. The seats are smoke-stained, with burns on the cloth between the thighs.

He flicks the ash from the tip of a Marlboro through the crack in the window and makes eye contact with a woman trudging her way through the snow past the bus stop. It looks like Ms. Nelson. He used to roam around with her son until the incident. It seems like yesterday they were teenagers sneaking beer into the football games and waltzing in tardy to fifth period—eyes bloodshot and glazed.

The truck suddenly swerves to the left. He overcorrects, sliding far to the right across snowy lanes. He nearly jumps the curb by the Post Office, but fortunately, the tires have just enough tread to regain traction. In a moment, he's back in the proper lane. The suspension's still there. So are the shocks. So are his reflexes, even dulled by the day drinking.

Rust has made a four-course meal of his '93 Ford Ranger. But the heat still works, and the radio crackles his favorite classics. He flips the dial. The numbers look fuzzy, but he makes out a nine up against a one next to an eight . . . or is it a three? Who knows? It's a neon blur. Better check the road.

"Safety first," he mumbles as if slurring it aloud adds points toward sobriety.

It must be an AM station, by the sound of all the talk and no tunes. He can't recall what he was listening to earlier—maybe something about the government or taxes. But there's a voice coming through the speakers—not Van Halen or AC/DC—but talk radio.

"The ten-year-old boy was found dead in a closet, wrapped up in a rug."

The next few lines continue:

"Cockroaches."

"Child protective services."

"He weighed thirty-four pounds."

"Mother arrested."

Pothole. The '93 Ranger leaps. Cans clink in unison.

"And now on to sports!"

He makes a wide—too-wide—fishtailing turn from Second Ave onto Greenhaven Drive. The tires finally grip in front of Old Lou's Books and the hardware store where Mike, his A.A. sponsor, sells a tool for any trouble.

He empties the beer he's been milking for the past ten minutes and crushes its midsection. With a flick of the wrist, he sets it free to join the rest. He turns down Dupont Street, past the hardware store, and with his thumb, he changes the frequency.

"Three women and eleven children were killed in an airstrike on a home in Afghanistan. Sources say it's not the—"

Static cuts through—

"The family—GRSHHS!—*collateral*—SHHFFT!—*embedded with hostil*—PSHHTT!"—interrupting any political commentary or spin.

He needs a beer. And cigs. He slips his last cigarette between his lips and zips the ninety-nine-cent lighter to a flame. The pack's empty now. But he can breathe again.

Johansson's Liquor Mart is two blocks to the east. He hunts for it. He stomps the accelerator and swerves his way through the streets, driving by Braille. As he speeds past the Feed Store, a voice cuts through the fuzz of static—

"And that's why, John, that we at the F.B.I. take every case seriously—follow up on every lead—so that when someone like our perpetrator here commits extensive identity fraud—we can nail 'em."

Six or seven neon signs hang in the window of Johansson's Liquor Mart. Budweiser glows red up against the green Rolling Rock horse. It makes everything look like Christmas again. Advertisements with jumbo letters cover up all the window space. Scantily clad cheerleaders stick to the window, promising everything but only delivering a trapdoor marketing campaign.

He flips up the collar on his denim company jacket and braces against the cold. It's embroidered with the letters: P-A-U-L. It's a good Christian name for an alcoholic who just lost his job. At least he got to keep the jacket. It does him little in the way of warmth against the cold, but it's just a moment before the bell above the door announces his arrival.

SlimJim's and margarita mix stand between him and the coolers with the cold beer. Corn nuts and Mountain Dew line his stupor. There's an A.T.M. on the opposite wall. To its left stands a grimy door with a faded sign:

"Restroom is for customers only."

Wouldn't you know? They're all out of Coors. He grabs the Budweiser twelve-pack instead.

"How 'bout uh couple them smokes there," Paul croaks as he points a yellow fingernail past the register.

"Yeah, no, the Marlboros. Yeah, the 100s."

The clerk stands behind the counter, a barbed wire tattoo wrapping up his arm. His eyes are glued to the TV. The thirteen-inch monitor's as heavy as a cinderblock and chained to the rafters. It's a wonder it still works—everything except the audio.

The nametag pinned to his polo reads *"JOSH,"* and above it, *"How may I help you?"* He looks anything but.

The store clerk reaches back for a pack of Marlboro Lights—like an owl with his eyes never leaving the "Breaking News!" It looks like a domestic issue. SWAT stands outside a mobile home, hunched behind shields, clad in Kevlar, creeping forward through the snow. The closed captions on the thirteen-inch spill out across the lower third of the screen:

"We're getting reports that an—
—ex-husband has barricaded himself in the—
—mobile home of his ex—
—wife with some children present—
—Sources tell us a seven-year-old boy and—
—a three-year-old girl are being held—
—at gunpoint."

The two men stare at the TV dangling from the ceiling until finally, Josh rings him up:

"$22.13."

Paul fishes a few wads from his pocket and proceeds to un-crinkle the greens on the glass display case. It shines back with five-dollar scratchers and a chance to win five thousand dollars. He shoves the bills toward the clerk. Paul figures he's either short or well over. After all, it's hard to compute with the buzz he's sustaining.

Should be a twenty and some fives in there, he thinks.

Josh returns the change with one eye stuck on the screen. SWAT breaches the door. A man lets loose a German shepherd straining at the leash. The K-9 bolts through the door, fur flying, fangs exposed, snapping his way into the mobile home. The dog disappears, and the TV looks frozen—a still frame. Until lightning strikes inside the trailer, strobing the curtains with a few short bursts.

The picture immediately cuts to the studio, where spray-tanned anchors can't conceal the horror. They fumble at any attempt to unsour the situation.

"Welp, I'll be damned," slurs Paul.

Josh returns to his unhelpful boredom.

"Thanks much," says Paul.

The store clerk nods. He watches Paul stumble past the stacks of magazines wrapped in plastic until he hears the door jingle.

Paul slams shut the door of his truck. He tears open the cardboard like a kid on Christmas and cracks open a fresh can. After guzzling its contents, he slips the key into the ignition and a fresh cigarette between his lips. The engine coughs and sputters, but the pistons fire up once again. He pulls out across snowy lanes onto Greenhaven Drive.

He's pretty tuned up after quickly making his way through a pair of Budweisers. The tires roll as he heads nowhere in particular. The road leads him to the outskirts of town, passing rows of houses and gnarled, naked trees.

With the polar vortex coming down, he figures he'll probably freeze to death in the beat-up truck. It'd be just his luck that the engine would cease, and he'd slide off into a snowy bank to shiver his life away.

It's not like he's living for much, truth be told. The job was keeping him six feet above ground anyway. Now that it's gone, what's the use?

He thinks back to the billboard he sees on his drive to work: *"Jesus is the WAY, the TRUTH, and the LIFE."* He thinks about it sometimes. But all the "Hail Marys" and "Our Father" hocus pocus stuff—just sounds like some fairy tale fiction for those who can't cope. Jesus on the cross is just a superstition. The way he sees it— you make your own way—play the cards you're dealt. If you need some "Jesus" to be your "*WAY,*" you're weak. If there is a "god," he's been long gone, Paul figures.

He spins a rickety U-turn across an empty snowy lane. The windshield wipers flap with a flurry. He figures he better stick to the town roads just in case. He doesn't want to die in the snow.

Maybe he'll stop in at Gino's and throwback a couple shots— shake off the cold? But the hard stuff always makes him sad. The ninety proof always brings him low, introspective and all. The morbid kind, though.

He'd probably start thinking about that garden hose—exhaust pipe—garage door closed. It's not the first time he thought about it.

The kid Mark, whose dad ran the shop, probably thought of it a thousand times. And then, on one thousand and one, his mother had to find him there in the garage, like a tire swing swaying in the summer breeze. In his basketball jersey. It broke the town. As much as Paul couldn't stand his boss, he felt for him. The kid was going through it, and in a way, Paul didn't blame him. He'd had the same thoughts.

They found the boss's kid on the same day, though. Ambulance, C.P.R., the whole works. He figures folks probably wouldn't find him for weeks, maybe months. A welfare check from some late-in-coming Good Samaritan would open his garage to find his truck out of gas, and the fumes lifted.

He turns the radio up to chase away the strategizing.

Left turn. Forward two blocks.

The sound of aluminum snaps as he cracks open another beer.

Right turn.

There's a bumper sticker on the van in front of him—"Take my hand, not my life"—with a baby looking sad and serious.

With the zip of a lighter, he sucks in air, working the cigarette.

Left turn, forward past the gas station.

He kicks himself, thinking, *Should've grabbed a few mags.* The ones sealed in plastic with airbrushed girls staring back. He could escape the loneliness for a moment.

Another right onto Park St.

The radio garbles:

"A seventeen-year-old female managed to flee from her captors Saturday morning in St. Cloud. Officers responded to Route 23 and Edgemont Drive, where they found the vict—"

Tired of driving, he switches off the AM noise. He turns off the street into a snowy parking lot. He idles in the cold and polishes off the rest of the can. The wipers scratch across the glass. He sees a sign between their passes: *St. John's Episcopal Church.* Suddenly, the wipers stop. The radio lights dim and go black. The engine coughs, sputters, and dies.

3

Pistis

THERE'S A THOUSAND-POUND FUTON in the spare bedroom which isn't much of a spare these days. But it's been spared for Roy's coming. He's been a friend of Margot and Sam since high school. Although time and space have separated them, his return to the west coast for the reunion has Margot and Sam eager in anticipation.

There's no extra space in the closet or garage, so hopefully, Roy can acclimate to a room strewn with alphabet puzzles and *Where's Waldo* books. Her son's Teenage Mutant Ninja Turtles line the dresser, and the stars glued to the ceiling illuminate the night. Perhaps Roy will return to his own boyhood.

It's a world away from the penthouse he's used to, she guesses. Margot ruminates on these things as she tucks in the dinosaur sheets with care. She folds a stack of brand-new towels—one hundred percent premium long-staple cotton. Three at least—bath, hand, and washcloth—were purchased for his occasion. Roy won't realize she ripped off the price tag and sent them through a quick wash cycle, but he would know if he saw their usual stained and fraying ones. Perhaps all her efforts may go unseen, but they certainly aren't wasted.

She sets the brand-new stack on the corner of the futon with fresh sheets. As she heads to the door, her feet make new prints on the vacuumed carpet. And there, she shuts it to preserve everything for Roy's arrival.

Margot dumps a scoop and a half into three ounces of warm water and shakes. The ten-pounder's fussy, but with a clean diaper and a belly full of formula, her entire world can instantly change. The bottle's not too hot or cold; it's just right. Margot tests it on her wrist just to be sure. Drops of formula spill across her veins. The nectar of little life—it's good. She tilts the bottle forty-five degrees upward. The baby's instincts kick in—suck, swallow, breathe—suck, swallow, breathe—like synchronized swimming or a well-oiled machine. That is until the thin whisp of air means the baby girl is through. Her mother lifts her vertically and taps, taps, taps with an open hand until a—"Burrrp!"—erupts inside her. Every three hours, like clockwork, her mother sustains her, filling her belly with life. It is the means to her survival, the substance of growth her parents and doctor all hoped for. And months from now, looking back, it'll be hard to believe how fast she's grown.

After laying the baby down beneath a mobile of stars and smiling shapes, Margot greases a nine-by-thirteen-inch dish and sets it aside. She whisks the cornmeal, flour, salt, and baking powder in a bowl and combines the corn, sour cream, and milk. Roy better not be lactose intolerant. Especially when it comes to the heart of her secret—she blends in the cheese, bacon, and jalapeños. He grew up in California, so she supposes he should be immune to the spice of jalapeños.

Margot doesn't use measuring spoons or cups—it's been ingrained in her over the years—and eyeballing it produces the best results. The battery substance blobs into the greased nine-by-thirteen and spreads to the four corners.

The baking dish enters the oven with a clang on the middle rack. The ingredients come together as expected for the next forty to forty-five until the center sets and the top is golden brown. Everything expands, and the baking powder works through the casserole like a mustard seed in good soil, producing thirty, sixty, or even a hundred times more goodness. The dishes pile up in the sink, but she and Sam have their ways figured out by now—if she cooks, he cleans, and if he cooks, she cleans. In the end, they both usually end up tag-teaming everything together.

A chime rings from the garage. The cycle's up. Jeans, t-shirts, socks, and underwear emerge from the dryer hot off the press. The lint trap gathers its fill. Sam always reminds her to clean it before starting the dryer, but she figures it's clean enough with him doing it every other time. The artificial scent of a lavender breeze fills the garage to mask the stench of gasoline and old sneakers.

She knows a lot of people who dread the laundry and how often it gathers in mountains around the house. But for Margot, there's a rhythmic beauty in the routine task, even in the mundane folding, sorting, moving, and storing. Her mother once told her, "Repetition strengthens and confirms," and she guesses it's true even with laundry. So, her trips back and forth with loads to launder and socks to match become a meditation of sorts—mindless wandering, but reflective, nonetheless.

With the new baby, it's been challenging for Margot and Sam to cover all the household chores. Fortunately, the square footage of the place is small enough that to vacuum and sweep, it only takes a moment. Getting started is another story, though. The bathrooms are small, but in the blur of days and weeks since they brought the baby home from the hospital, cleaning the toilets has been a low priority. But with Sam picking up Roy at the airport today, the motivation's all there. She dons rubber gloves, gathers a scrub brush, and with a bleachy concoction, she scours the porcelain. Margot thinks of an article from the *Times* with the lookalike lungs of chain smokers and non-smoking housekeepers. She holds her breath.

For a month now, Margot's been on maternity leave. It's still awkward not going into the office. Call it cabin fever or being antsy, but it's got her going. She feels drawn to accomplishing the little tasks here and there, especially the sort that helps her coworkers feel less of a pinch in her absence. It's this little bit extra that she's always been known for. Her coworkers love her. Maybe it's her perseverance? Her attitude and approach? Perhaps it's the courage to shatter glass ceilings for herself and those around her.

A lot of the inspiration comes from her mother. The woman worked two jobs to keep food in the fridge and a roof over their head. Hers is the story of countless mothers—a single mom without child support. It wasn't until Margot was in high school that her mom could scale back to one full-time job. And in it, she rose through the ranks. It wasn't that her mom crushed the competition; she was just better. She had a dogged determination like her life depended on it—because it did.

Margot phones her every afternoon at 2:30. Her mother's retired now, and she always looks forward to their afternoon chats. There's no agenda for their conversation, but it typically turns into something meaningful. It always ends with a simple, slow phrase:

"I love you so . . . so . . . much."

Margot knows these phone calls won't last forever, so she savors them daily.

The mailbox is stuffed with three days' worth of junk mail and bills. On Margot's way in from the box, she rifles through the mess. It turns out it's not all junk and bills. There are some worthy causes sent her way through the post. She sifts through the paperwork and all the decisions that come with it. Decisions about a new garage door or sending funds to an orphan in Tanzania—for a goat, a cow, or chickens for his community. Decisions about real estate, diet plans, or eligibility for hearing aids—all stuffed in her box. What's most essential, she figures, is what informs her decision-making.

The smartphone buzzes in her back pocket. She shuffles the mail to the other hand, retrieves the phone, and swipes to answer.

"Hey, love," Margot mumbles into the phone, cradling the cell between her ear and shoulder.

"Hey, just wanted to check in," says Sam, "Gonna have to circle around again. I guess Roy's flight just got in. Delayed a bit."

"All right, I'll see you in a few then."

"Love you," says Sam.

"Love you too," Margot replies.

But the whining brakes of an oncoming bus drown out her words. Fortunately, there's no follow-up sound of smashing metal. A few years ago, she would've dialed Sam right back, fearing the worst—that he wouldn't pick up. She'd be breathless with her heart pulsing, franticly asking Sam if he was all right. Her hands would be trembling, and she'd drop the mail into a sink full of dishes. That was after the accident.

It took her a while to get behind the steering wheel again. One day though, she did. After three surgeries and a reconstructed pelvis, she was finally doing it.

She had never dreamed of it, especially when she looked up from the wreckage of a crushed can that used to be a four-door sedan. The airbags hung out, limp like a dog's tongue on a hot day. The cars were pressed nose to nose and thank God it wasn't blood—it was radiator fluid bleeding out and snaking across the asphalt.

The scene crawled with bystanders, paramedics, and police officers in reflective vests. In the blue and red flashing deep in the night, an officer scribbled eyewitness statements with his pen and pad. Another passed by, trailing behind him a distance-measuring wheel. Firefighters ripped open the ribcages of the cars. Flashlights blinded her eyes. A neck brace choked her, and her skull was sinched into the plastic stretcher.

Everything was shattered. It's a wonder Margot made it out. Physical therapy was ruthless, but therapists must be if you expect to walk again.

What she did not expect was that a year and a half later, she'd be expecting. Driving was less of an ordeal by then. She had slowly made headway through her trauma. Often it was two steps forward and one or two back. But on the horizon, the uncertainty of pregnancy and a reconstructed pelvis loomed heavy. And yet, after everything, she had not expected what she was experiencing—the living, walking, driving, birthing. Each was a mountain in its own way, but sometimes mountains can move. It's what she continues to believe now, eight years on and two babies since—sometimes mountains can move. For her, it's a repetition that strengthens and confirms.

4

Qadosh

PAUL BARNES STANDS BESIDE the wooden sign: *St. John's Episcopal Church*. The engine won't turn over—out of gas, or finally, the engine gave out. He drops his spent cigarette into the snow. With the sole of his steel toe, he stubs out the final glow of wisping ash. It's not like he's saving the town from a brushfire; it's merely a natural reflex.

There are too many cars in the parking lot, he thinks, *especially for a Saturday, hell, even a Sunday.* It's not like he's familiar with the parking lot on Sundays, but he can't imagine it'd be this full. Maybe it's just the illusion of multiplying cars—fuzzy images induced by one too many beers. He's not even sure how he ended up here.

It's freezing outside, and his knees are knocking, so he staggers up the icy steps and through the huge oaken doors to St. John's. Through the doors, he's hit—sucker-punched and nearly floored. Perhaps it's the warmth, the glow, or the framed photo of the kid in the casket, but it steals his breath. It's Mark, his boss's son. He'd seen his picture displayed in the boss's office in the machine shop, but it's strange seeing it here beside the casket. The blood vessels dilated from his day drinking constrict. It feels like something between a heart attack and electrocution. It has him struck stone-cold sober. What was he doing here?

The choir members look like ghosts past the wooden pews of coats and dresses. The priests or whatever dressed in white robes waft smoke around, filling the cavern with incense or magic.

There's a purity about the place. It has Paul stopped in his tracks. His legs feel frozen, like he's still outside in the snow. He loiters in the doorway of the church, wondering: *Should I stand? Or sit? Or bow? Or turn and leave?*

Maybe it's the stained-glass windows, the melting candles, or the heart-aching people, but there's something electric in his bones and all over his skin.

The pipe organ sweeps through the room, clearing the cobwebs and dusting the colored glass with an ethereal melody. A wave of white rises, their robes bleached without blemish. And with one voice, they sing:

"Be still, my soul; the Lord is on your side;

bear patiently the cross of grief or pain;

leave to your God to order and provide;

in ev'ry change he faithful will remain.

Be still, my soul; your best, your heav'nly friend

through thorny ways leads to a joyful end."

It all looks and sounds foreign to Paul. He reminds himself, though—these voices belong to ordinary folks from the community—Mrs. Elba, the postmaster; Annie, Mike's wife from the hardware store; Cedric from the bowling alley. They're just singing out different notes to the tune of an oversized, gaudy piano. But to his ear and heart and something deeper, it's like the sound of heaven touching earth.

The choir continues to fill the room full of sorrow with the resolve of "being forever with the Lord." Their voices hope for some occasion when "disappointment, grief, and fear are gone" and how "we shall meet at last."

It's something he's never seen, never experienced in his life. As if the ordinary, mundane things are suddenly transformed into something otherworldly. Or perhaps the otherworldly was always there in the mundane and ordinary, and he never saw it before?

"I am Resurrection and I am Life, says the Lord."

Well, it's actually a priest. She lifts her eyes from the pages and speaks in tones that echo off the stone walls:

"Whoever has faith in me shall have life, even though they die."

She hangs on the last three letters, sending spiders up his spine.

"And everyone who has life, and has committed themselves to me in faith, shall not die forever."

At this, Paul's thoughts swirl. Memories rush back. He sees his grandma's face sunken and caked with makeup at the mortuary. Then there's Eugene on the TV screen dressed up in his Marine Corps class A's. And Marty's empty eyes staring back at him. He sees the clam chowder across his blue skin and the mess of pills on the floor. The deaths they died feel like forever ago. They haunt him still. His grandma's funeral was just a blur at the mortuary. For Eugene and Marty, he was a no-show. This is something more. There's a substance to it, a mystery unlocking itself inside of him, bringing him close. To what? He's not quite sure.

In the pews, mothers rummage through their purses for tissues. Arched backs of boys and men trying to be men strain as stiff as washboards. They suffocate every nerve to collapse into tears. Instead, they sigh, quickly wipe their eyes, and cough to shake off emotions.

The woman in white continues:

"In the midst of life, we are in death; from whom can we seek help?"

Suddenly, he's a fourteen-year-old boy standing beside the doorstep, afraid to cross the threshold and find his mother lifeless. His unmoved feet created channels in the porch as police, paramedics, and coroners shuttled in and out. They rolled her out after what felt like a week. As she wheeled by, encased in thick plastic with a zipper down the middle, he could not move a muscle. He was mute to mouth any word.

The voices of the bereaved erupt:

"Holy God, Holy and Mighty, Holy and merciful Savior, deliver us not into the bitterness of eternal death."

Their tongues sound tied, though, as if the truth of their words has a hard time coming.

"O God, whose beloved Son took children into his arms and blessed them: Give us the grace to entrust Mark to your never-failing care and love, and bring us all to your heavenly kingdom; through Jesus Christ our Lord, who lives and—"

—A hand rests on his shoulder.

Is that you, God? Paul questions in the silence of his thoughts. *Never really heard much about you growing up except for "dammit" and "bless America." Well, it's not entirely true. I did pray when mom got sick. But no one listened. She just got worse.*

A voice sounds in his ear—a whisper:

"Excuse me, sir, we, uh, have a seat over here if you'd like to sit down?"

"Oh, uh, sure, yeah," says Paul, waking up.

The usher helps him to the end of a pew beside a full-length collage of colored glass. To Paul's left in the window, a glowing man with an orb around his head stares into a dark cave. At the edge of the cave stands a pale, sorry attempt of a person. The light pierces through to produce vibrant reds, yellows, and greens that dull the figure haunting the cave. With everyone's eyes facing forward at a framed photo of the kid in the casket, Paul's are up and to the left. What is it about this glass? This man and this cave? It moves beneath his skin.

"And he will destroy on this mountain the shroud that is cast over all peoples, the sheet that is spread over all nations; he will swallow up death forever. Then the Lord God will wipe away the tears from all faces . . . "

The pipe organ echoes a tone that is rich and haunting. The wave of white rises, and with their hearts more than their lips, they sing:

Holy, holy, holy! Lord God Almighty!
Early in the morning, our song shall rise to thee.
Holy, holy, holy, merciful, and mighty!
God in three persons, blessed Trinity!
Holy, holy, holy! All the saints adore thee,
casting down their golden crowns around the glassy sea;
cherubim and seraphim falling down before thee,
which wert and art and evermore shalt be.

Holy, holy, holy! Though the darkness hide thee,
though the eye of sinful man thy glory may not see,
only thou art holy; there is none beside thee,
perfect in pow'r, in love, and purity.
Holy, holy, holy! Lord God Almighty!
All thy works shall praise thy name in earth, and sky and sea.
Holy, holy, holy! Merciful and mighty!
God in three persons, blessed Trinity!

The experience is dream-like—not like a drunken spell—but like his first rollercoaster. It's exhilarating, with his heart thumping through his ribs. Navy Pier, it was, in Chicago. His dad was nursing a hangover, draped outside over the railing, staring at ice rafts on Lake Michigan. But inside, with all the rollercoasters—lights and sounds and jerking machines, Paul's little body was jolted from the doldrums of a midwestern existence.

After the choir, an ordinary soul begins to speak. He clears his throat and introduces himself as:

"Xavier Simmons, ahem. . .but better known as 'Coach.'"

His words aren't poetic or religious but heartfelt and set apart. They're what you might expect to hear on wooden courts and in humid locker rooms.

"Mark was such a team player. Hard worker. Stubborn like an ox but dogged like a bull."

Coach doesn't shuffle through notecards. He doesn't flip through stapled papers. He also doesn't shy away from the truth of Mark's fatal decision with an extension cord tied to garage rafters and a note saying "Sorry." Of course, he doesn't detail it like that—such was already common knowledge of the town—but he doesn't shy away from saying "suicide." The term comes out shivery and most likely not what the teenage boy's parents wanted. But Coach knows that sugarcoating has no place when life is on the line.

Coach Xavier addresses the problem his power forward Mark may have faced—and how it might be the same issue that others suffer. He lays out the struggle like x's and o's on a dry-erase board. And with a coach's guilt for wishing he could've done more, he tries to do more for others.

"We might never fully understand why Mark decided to do what he did, but I want you to know—that your life matters. Who you are and the struggle you're in—it matters. And don't think for a second you're all alone in this."

Next to the dead man walking in the stained glass, Paul feels drawn to the coach's strategy and vision. It's a finding for what he's been searching for, even though he never knew he was searching. There's a purity present, as Coach continues—

"Best part about a team—you got others at your side."

Coach wipes his eyes, turns to the royal blue casket—and mouths the word "Goodbye."

After four verses of *It Is Well With My Soul*, there's another reading about separations of death and life and angels and rulers, and a whole bunch more made impossible. Paul listens expectantly to some words everyone recites in unison—with pauses in all the proper places. They utter about a father named "hallowed" whose kingdom comes, whose will is done. There's talk of daily bread and forgiveness—and that's where things sound muddled for a moment as the word comes out "debt-passes." And right around the corner comes evil, temptation, and deliverance.

It's quite the pledge of allegiance, Paul thinks to himself. They don't quite sound happy as they say it, but they sound firm with every word, even if it rolls off the tongue mindlessly. There's something there in them that's not there in Paul. Or not yet.

His worn-out Wranglers feel glued to the pew, even after boys in matching royal blue jerseys carry the coffin out. He sits there until the room clears. The cavern of the church looks a lot bigger now that it's empty. The sunlight pours through the colored glass, more vibrant and expansive, not caught by coats and dresses. There's a scene of a cross and friends nearby. Fish and baskets of bread. A sheep and a lion.

It's all a mystery to him. Layers of meaning to be uncovered. How can the ordinary, the mundane, be transformed so electrically? So otherworldly?

He reaches into his breast pocket for the Marlboros. He's not sure if he can light up here, but he figures the priest already smoked up the place, so what the hell? He's got things to think about. A new world of possibility awaits him.

Either he's ditching the '93 Ranger to fill up on beer, or he's sitting here for a while—next to the pale glass man peeking from a cave, amongst the empty pews and a framed picture of a boy whose story could mirror his.

5

Chara

HE KNOCKS ON THE door of apartment twenty-seven. A pause. Five seconds, ten seconds. His knuckles rattle again against the wood. The interval's patient, though; the weight of the knocks politely measured. It's a night and day difference from the pounding of SWAT or U.S. Marshals frequenting the complex. Fifteen seconds, twenty. He knocks a third time, rattling off four heavier beats. As he reaches for a fourth, suddenly, the door swings open. And there in the doorway shines his mother's wide smile with her gold molars beaming.

Her skin sags. Time draws new lines, claiming its due early on. There's a breath of silence between them. The only sound is the hiss of oxygen shooting up her nostrils. The tank at her side is topped in green and stickered with "Warning"—"Compressed Oxygen"—"Flammable."

Xavier steps forward and wraps his arms around the skin and bones that vaguely resembles his mother. Her skeletal frame is draped in a nightgown sprouting with rose blossoms. The gown stretches to the floor and hangs over the ears of discolored bunny slippers.

"Glad you came, honey," she says as she cradles his head.

"It's been a day, Mama," Xavier exhales.

"Well, come on in," she says, "don't let the heat out now."

As Xavier closes the door and steps into the cramped apartment, he notices the stubbed-out Newports in a coffee mug on the windowsill. The ghost of cigarettes past still haunts the air.

"You know, Mama, you ain't supposed to be smoking—with the cancer and all. Especially with the uh . . . " he points to the oxygen tank beside her.

"Oh, hush now," she waves him off, "it was just one . . . for old time's sake. I'm doing just fine, don't you worry. Come sit down now," she motions for him to take a seat at the kitchen table.

Xavier threads his way through the apartment, passing framed pictures of every stage of his basketball journey. Behind another glass, his father stands at attention in military greens. And in the photo beside it, his sister Crystal cradles a new baby. He moves a stack of magazines off a chair and sets them on the table beside three others.

"Coffee?" his mother asks.

"Yes, ma'am," answers Xavier.

He places the mug atop a National Geographic titled: "The Truth About Black Holes."

He clears his throat and says,

"You know, you could save some cash each month just canceling some of these."

Xavier shuffles through a stack of magazines featuring "Jaguars," "Tornadoes," and "Everyday Mindfulness: Finding Focus, Calm, and Joy."

"Well, where would I go? Ever since Lucky's, I've been here. How can I know about Egypt if I can't go there? Like they say: 'You might be poor, your shoes might be broken, but your mind is a palace,'" she chuckles.

"Sure, Mama."

"It's the little things, you know?" she continues, "Makes a difference. Like see, here . . . just learned this morning."

She thumbs through an edition featuring the possibility of life on Mars.

"Here," she says proudly between the ticks of incoming oxygen. Following her index finger, she reads aloud:

"Deep-sea octopus's eggs take over five years to hatch."

"Okay . . . great?" laughs Xavier tiredly.

His mother shushes him, not to be interrupted:

"Their mother does not leave, *even* to eat," she stresses the word, "and then she *dies* when the larvae hatch—I mean, imagine that! All that work and then gone."

She gazes at her son, amazed.

"Sounds like coaching high school ball," laughs Xavier.

"I bet." They laugh and smile.

Her voice softens, and she sighs,

"How'd it go today, honey? Wish I could've been there for you. And the town too."

Her eyes fall to the canister at her side. It's mobile, but she's not. Going from the register at Lucky's to the confines of a one-bedroom apartment has been abrupt and unbearable. "Cancer's a devil," that's what she says.

"I guess it went just as you might expect," says Xavier between sips of coffee.

"It's just . . ." he pauses, "different with kids, though," he continues, "they're so new to stuff like loss. It hits, and it hurts, you know?"

He looks away, holding back tears, straining every muscle around his eyes to focus on anything else. The year-round Nativity trinkets beside the TV do the trick.

"Just so heavy, you know?" he chokes.

"Mm-hmm," she pauses. "I grew up with a boy in Jackson who died when we were teenagers. Just about tore my heart in two. Not saying, 'I get it,' but I know it hurts."

They exhale a weight heavier than their breath. A pause. Ten seconds, fifteen. In the hiss of oxygen, they scan the room for a change of subject.

"You hungry?"

"Yes, ma'am," Xavier smiles.

"Let me see what I can fix up real quick. Got a minute?"

"Oh, I got time, Mama."

"Good."

Xavier loosens his tie, relaxing the stiff nature of the suit, and watches his mother search through the fridge.

"Let's see," she says, with her head in the door, "how about some leftover cornbread and honey chicken?"

"That'd be just fine. Love me something sweet!" Xavier says across the linoleum. "Hey," he smiles, "remember when you lit the house on fire baking peach cobbler?" Xavier laughs.

"I most certainly did not!" she snaps, hands on her hips, a smile cracking through.

"Oh yes, you did! If it wasn't for Crystal waking you up, we would've been out on the streets!"

"Nonsense," she laughs, "I was just resting my eyes. Besides, a little toasted peaches ain't gonna hurt nobody."

"A little? Uh-huh?"

They laugh aloud until the microwave dings. The cornbread and chicken steam in a world of radiation.

"You know," says Xavier, receiving the leftovers, "I saw Mrs. Davis at the funeral today. She asked after you. Told me they've got the whole church praying for you over at First Baptist."

"That's sweet of her."

"Yeah, I guess her grandson is close with Mark—sorry—*was* close with Mark . . . you know, the boy . . . who uh . . . died."

"Anyway," says Xavier, "she said her grandson's gonna start some club at school for suicide prevention. Depression. 'Not Again' or 'Not One More' or something. Good kid."

There's a loud thump from the ceiling above. It's followed by heavy stomping. Xavier's eyes dart upward. The lamp dangling over the kitchen table sways and the cabinets tremble. His mother seems unfazed. As she readjusts her nasal cannula, ensuring the flow of oxygen, Xavier asks, desperately—

"Why do you put up with this, Mama?"

"Oh, I don't. That's nothing. Should've heard it two weeks ago. It must've been New Year's Eve, I guess? Like a wrecking ball tearing through the place. He's screaming, Rosa's crying. Crashing sounds. I hear the kids sobbing through the walls."

"You gotta be kidding me."

"I bumped into her in the hall. Her eyes were swollen beneath her sunglasses. I saw bruising around her wrist when she reached for the mail."

"What'd you tell her?"

"I said, honey, a man who treats you like that is no man at all."

"What about telling the cops? Get a restraining order or something?"

"Says she doesn't want to press charges. Says he gets worked up sometimes, but she knows he loves her."

Xavier shook his head in disbelief.

"More common than you know, son."

She pauses for a moment, weighing her next words, and says—

"I saw him going up the stairs the other day—her husband. So, I yelled after him. Said, 'there's a reckoning coming if you lay your hands on her again!'"

Xavier drops the chicken—

"Mama, you gotta be careful—"

"—I ain't afraid of him!" she says, standing up and wheeling her oxygen to the kitchen.

"Whoa, okay! Look out! Here comes Sugar Ray Leonard!" Xavier laughs, masking the worry.

After he cleaned every bone and each crumb from his plate, Xavier says,

"You know, the kids really get scarred seeing all that. Everybody says they're so resilient, but, well, with Mark, I don't think so. Not so much."

"Mm-hmm," she agrees.

"Y'all was pretty resilient after your dad, you know ... but ... "

Her voice trails off.

Fifteen seconds, twenty.

She shuffles forward, coffee pot in one hand, oxygen in the other.

"Refill?" It rolls off her lips like she's back at Lucky's.

She did more than tend the register there. Coffee pick-me-ups were her favorite part of the breakfast routine. It was her greatest joy to caffeinate the customers, warming them up for the day ahead.

"Sure, thanks," says Xavier. "I gotta have a meeting with the players and their parents ... the AD and the higher-ups ... you know, what are we gonna do about the rest of the season? After all, the chemistry changes. There's his empty locker, new shoes to fill."

"Most important thing—just be there for the boys. The change comes with heartache, but maybe with it, new opportunities too. What I always believed anyway."

She sets the coffee pot back in its warmer and sits beside him at the table, the tank between them.

"I tell you 'bout Miss Johnson? You know, the grocer? Lives a few doors down?"

"No, what's up?" Xavier asks.

"Had her red Nissan stolen right there off the curb."

"You know, Mama," he takes her boney hand in his, "you can always come live with us—"

"—No, this is my home! I ain't leaving," she says defiantly. "Anyway, they found it—the Nissan—crashed out in a cornfield off the interstate, burnt to a crisp—like that cobbler," she laughs.

"That's terrible," says Xavier shaking his head.

"You know what she said?—'Stuff ain't everything.' Just laughed it off. Said—'Thanks for taking it off my hands—someone should've torched it long ago,'" she laughs deep, hacking at her lungs.

"You alright?"

"I'm fine, I'm fine," she shoos him away.

But her frail body continues its decline. Looking close, Xavier can see the rows of her ribs through the nightgown. Her eyes look yellow and tired. She stands up again, wiping her lips on a napkin, and shuffles her bunny slippers back to the coffee pot. The wheel of the oxygen tank catches on her chair and almost sends her sprawling across the floor. But a strong pull does the trick, and the tank frees. Returning with a half-empty pot, she asks,

"More coffee? Warmup, at least?"

"Yes, ma'am."

She smiles as she pours, the gold caps on her molars reflecting the overhead lamp. But as she moves her eyes from the cup to her boy, her pour splashes across the table.

"Oh, shoot! Sorry, hun! You okay?" she fusses.

"I'm fine, Mama, I'm fine," he reassures her.

Xavier rises, untouched by the scalding coffee. But the same could not be said of a half-year's worth of National Geographics. Portraits of orangutangs and space shuttles sop up the spill. As

Xavier dabs the table and magazines with a rag, he lifts the stack beneath his mug to find past-due bills and final notices stamped in red.

"Uh . . . Mama, what's this?"

"Oh, it's nothing, honey."

"Says it's from the electric company? This one *here* . . . " he unearths a yellow envelope, "says it's the gas? Mama, you gotta tell me these things. It's a final notice! Can't have you shivering here in the cold!"

"It's fine, honey. Everything's just fine."

It's not like Lucky's had a retirement package. Social Security keeps food in the fridge and most of the bills at bay, but the funds aren't there with the rent climbing, the chemo, and the mass of medical payoffs. But she says it decisively—

"The Lord will provide. He always does. Ram in a thicket if it has to be."

"But Mama, it doesn't have to be like this. We don't want you to struggle. I mean, how long can you keep on doing this?"

"Long as I can. Really, *it's fine*, honey. Don't want you to worry."

"But it *does* worry me, Mama. Doesn't have to be so hard, you know?"

A pause. Five seconds, ten.

She looks her son square in the eyes.

Fifteen seconds, twenty.

With the hiss of oxygen shooting up into her nostrils and down into her failing lungs, she says—

"I read somewhere—joy is the oxygen for doing hard things."

6

Tov

"REALLY, SAM? A MINIVAN?"

Sam laughs, "Yeah, sorry, this is your limo service. Had to drop the kids off at school on my way down."

No wonder the car smells like rotting chicken nuggets and fermented baby formula. At least it explains the French fries ground into the seats and the Cheerios across the floorboards.

"How was the flight?" Sam asks, glancing over at his old friend.

"Tell you the truth, it was miserable. Just miserable," Roy says as he adjusts his expensive Ray-Bans.

"Wow. Really?" asks Sam.

"Yeah, people nowadays! No respect! Like, c'mon, you gotta be kidding me! This is *first class*, and the stewardess—flight attendant—Janet or whatever—can't even make a decent rum and coke."

He pauses for dramatic effect, looking over at Sam as if to gather his support on the absurdity of it all and continues:

"And then—this is all before they let the entire zoo in—Janet or whatever says she's '*So sorry*' and would, '*in a jiff*, remake it if that's all right?' Well, all hell breaks loose before she brings it back. They let the zoo in—snot-nosed kids with their nasty hands touching everything. Overweight, incompetent parents glazed over munching on Big Macs. And then—get this—they slam their bags across every row. Some broad even spilled my warm nuts!"

"Wow, man, sounds rough," replies Sam, keeping his eyes on the road.

"Yeah, it's not like it's *business class*—it's *first class, have some respect!*"

But Roy won't let it go:

"And then we land—and Janet or whatever—tries to cozy up, as if her second or third cocktails improved an inch—'hope you had a pleasant flight, Mr. Macomber?'" he mocks.

Sam merges the minivan onto the CA-1 and takes the coastal route northward. The lunchtime traffic's not any better, but the view is. Between motels with "Free HBO" marquees and used car lots, they catch glimpses of the sea.

"How's Chicago?" Sam asks, eager to change the subject.

"Cold. Icy. Dreadful."

"Thought you enjoyed it out there?" asks Sam, looking over.

"Well, yeah, of course. Business is great, cash is flowing. I aim to close out one of the best quarters on record. Bought a vacation spot up at the lake, you know, a little getaway cabin for some R&R."

"Oh boy, I know about needing R&R," laughs Sam, "love her to death, but baby girl's keeping us all up at night—she's colicky, so it's tough to get a wink of sleep. Think we'll get through it, though . . . someday."

"Yeah, so anyways," interrupts Roy, "we've got this new quota we're trying to reach and an updated profit margin to increase the shareholders' equity. And of course, there's new competition smelling blood in the water, so we're clamping down, putting in hours, double-crossing the 't's' and double dotting the 'i's' if you know what I mean?"

"Sure, sure," says Sam, who's clueless about quarters, profit margins, and shareholders' equity. He's a high school history teacher on paternity leave. But he tries to sound interested because it's Roy.

The Pacific Coast Highway hugs the seashore, and multimillion-dollar homes dangle off the cliffs. Further north, the traffic eases, and the one-lane road opens up. Sam eases his grip on the wheel and cruises along.

"I'm thrilled you came, Roy. I still can't believe it's our twentieth reunion."

"Well, I had the trip to Key West last week. D.C. is next. Lined up just right, I guess, so I thought, what the hell?"

"Margot has the room fixed up real nice for you. Sure, it's a futon . . . but uh . . . no amount of money could take it off my hands—never had a better night's sleep. I even think Margo's making her world-famous cornbread casserole for dinner. Kids can't wait to see you too!"

"Oh yeah, about that. Uh, well, I figured I'd have my secretary put me up at the Four Seasons. It's where I stay for all my travel."

"Oh, okay, uh . . . yeah, sure, man, that's fine," Sam replies, a little taken aback. But cheerfully, he stammers,

"Well, dinner will be great, though!"

"Yeah, yeah, we'll have to see," answers Roy, open-ended.

They pass the Getty Villa with its tranquil gardens and ocean breezes. Sam glances over to Roy.

"Hey, uh, I just wanted to say," Sam begins, his voice soft and low, "we're all really sorry about your dad. I know he was a tough man. I remember him yelling and making us run extra laps. But I know he had a good heart too. Like the time he helped my mom fix the water heater after my parents split, he was so quic—"

"—Sorry, gotta take this."

The iPhone hums in his cashmere sport coat until Roy slips it out.

"What?!" he says, more of a rebuke than a question. "Yes, Jessica. I told you a thousand times! With the present market tanking, privatization is key in negotiating an optimum operating profit/loss value . . ."

Roy trails off in the foreign language of business.

Sam once took a five-unit Macro and Microeconomics course in college, but it was a rudimentary General Ed. requirement for the history department. His college plan was more about landing some job—any job—that would make it possible for him to marry Margot. And, of course, he wanted to help people—be an influence, a positive role model for the kids. They're the next generation, after all. It wasn't about the paycheck (other than making ends meet); it was about the passion. He saw his job like a seed that produces an orchard. And there's that quote from Maya Angelou that always stuck with him:

"At the end of the day, people won't remember what you said or did; they will remember how you made them feel."

He could care less about their beat-up minivan if it kept his family safe and got them from point A to B and back again.

"It's about managing the optics," Roy continues, "Just ballpark it, Jessica, dammit! Then circle back when you've got what I want!"

Roy hangs up without saying "Thanks" or "Bye now." He exhales—

"*Je-sus!* Some people, am I right?!"

Sam just looks over at his old friend in his pricey tailored suit.

As they snake around the dead grassy cliffs, dodging the shining sea, Roy points across the dash to a three-story new construction suspending off the cliffs.

"Bet I could seal the deal on something like that—nice to have a vacation home out west. How much do you think they go for nowadays?"

"Oh, I wouldn't even know," says Sam, whose three-bedroom, two-bath rental keeps climbing.

"I'd say three, three point five, maybe four mill. Maybe a cash offer'll sweeten the deal, and I can get away with a solid three."

"Wow, yeah, sure," says Sam, unimpressed.

A moment of silence moves between them as the minivan passes a sign on the side of the road: *Malibu 27 Miles of Scenic Beauty.*

"So, how's the love life, bro? Plan on settling down any time soon?" asks Sam.

"No, definitely not. Don't get me wrong, the love life's popping. But get tied down? Nah, that's not for me. The business—I live and breathe it—twenty-four seven, three sixty-five. I mean, look at you. You got the kids and Margot. Are you really satisfied? At the end of the day, Sam, are you?"

"Yeah, I mean, for sure. Wouldn't trade it for the world."

"That's what they all say," Roy balks, "until the money dries up and someone gets caught sleeping around."

"Nah, man, I really feel like we're doing it," says Sam. "Every day's a new adventure—changing and growing up, you know? Not just me and Margot, but all of us. Just kind of fall in love with 'em more each day, you know? 'Course, there's the highs and lows, but love and commitment keep you going in the end."

"Yeah, okay." Roy fiddles with his phone—responding to texts and emails with both thumbs firing away. Then abruptly, he looks up and interjects—

"About that dinner, yeah, sorry, I have a face-to-face with a potential client."

There was almost a hint of remorse in his "sorry."

"All good, man."

Sam's disappointment is present, and he grows a little less surprised at the letdown. Still, he figures at least they can all enjoy the reunion together. Sam turns the conversation to old times.

"So, you keep up with anybody from high school? I still see the usual suspects, you know, Chris and Andrew, Simone. I actually teach with Chris—he's a geometry and algeb—"

"—Wasn't Simone the black chick whose dad blew his brains out?" interrupts Roy.

"Uh, yeah. It was pretty tragic. Think it was PTSD after his time in the military. She's sure bounced back, though—a social worker now. Our kids play socc—"

"—Yeah, she was pretty hot back in the day. Wonder if she let herself go?"

"I don't know, man. Simone and her husband Dave have been great friends over the years."

Sam continues, "You ever keep up with your cousin Paul? The one from Minnesota, is it? I'll never forget that summer he came out."

"No. He's probably wasting his life away somewhere," sighs Roy.

Roy pulls the iPhone from his breast pocket and fires his fingers away at the screen. And then, suddenly, he stops.

"What the?" he says, "what is this, Timbuktu? No service?"

"Oh, yeah, sorry, with the canyons and all, the service drops in this part. It's a beautiful section, though, worth the drop if you ask me.

The minivan twists through the canyons. Out the passenger window, iron netting stretches up the slope, in hopes of boulders staying put, or at the very least, out of the roadway. The driver's side shows a sliver of the endless sea, with swells rolling in from the south. Pelicans glide across the water with their feathers skimming the surface. A pod of dolphins bobs up for air as they sift through the kelp beds a hundred yards offshore. It's what you might miss with the faintest bit of cell service.

Yet Roy struggles relentlessly to manufacture a cell tower's notice of his importance. He misses every bit of beauty and manages only to look up from his screen when he feels the minivan slow.

"What, you need to take a leak or something? Outta gas?" he chuckles to himself.

The minivan slows and grumbles off the asphalt onto a dusty narrow shoulder. Sam pulls up behind a Honda Civic with its emergency lights flashing and hood up. Textbook indication of car trouble, just like the DMV handbook.

"Sam, c'mon, you gotta be kidding me?"

"Nah, man, they need some help. There's no service here. Who knows how long it'll take AAA or CHP to find 'em?"

"What're you some 'Good Samaritan' now?"

"No, just trying to do the right thing, man. Look, it'll be quick. I bet it's just a blown tire."

Sam puts the minivan in park and kills the ignition.

"You can stay if you want. It'll just be a second."

"Whatever, man," Roy spits, irritated.

The distance between the minivan and the edge of the road is tight. So, Sam checks his mirror and over his shoulder before jetting out the door. With his head on a swivel, he jogs up behind the Civic, checking behind for oncoming traffic.

Inside the minivan, Roy sits, growing more unamused by the minute. He triple-checks the *"No Service"* notification on his phone and skims through past texts and emails. After some time, Roy sees Sam beside the teenager reaching into the trunk of the Civic and emerging with a rubber spare. Sam hands the teenager the tire iron while carrying the scissor jack over to the blowout.

"C'mon man, what the hell?!" Roy says aloud to the empty car seats of the minivan.

"What is *this*?! Auto-shop now? Father-son bonding?!"

His Italian leather shoes hit the ground with fury. He doesn't even take time to button up the cashmere sport coat as he stomps his way to the Good Samaritan and three-tired Civic.

The horn of a work truck rings in his ears.

"Dammit, Sam! What's taking so—"

7

Elpis

"Get here fast. *You're going to be a dad.*"

He read the text message over the kitchen sink, but the words didn't register.

She had endured four sleepless nights—acid reflux, heartburn, the works. They dialed the on-call nurse around midnight, and she relayed instructions about the proper dosage of an antacid for pregnancy.

But by the morning, there was still no relief, so she came for a check-up. She was seven months pregnant and waddled her way up the stairs to the OBGYN's office. By the time the doctor finally walked into the room, her husband was across town, pulling into the hardware store parking lot. He felt the phone vibrate in the middle of the plumbing section. He picked up, and his wife said,

"They're sending me to the hospital . . . I guess my numbers—protein numbers, the nurse said—are high."

A few hours later, she was clothed in a hospital gown, laid in a bed with wheels, and stuck with an IV full of magnesium. The machines beeped and monitored the peaks and valleys of both their hearts. His utero heart ran faster, but hers was dangerously catching up thanks to an emerging condition called *preeclampsia*. Her blood pressure soared to an all-time high. Her skin felt clammy and turned cherry red. How the nurses described it, it's like she was becoming allergic to the baby.

Her husband headed home to grab a few things since they'd be calling the hospital home for the next few days. Exiting the automatic glass doors, he phoned his grandmother about watching the dog. He texted their neighbors Sam and Margot about grabbing the mail. He called his boss and explained how he'd be out for a few days, one to two at the most, he hoped.

At home, he grabbed a snack and packed a few things. The house they had renovated was still in remodeling mode. They had just moved in a few months before, but the place was sparsely furnished, the future baby room empty of a crib and bare of decor.

The phone vibrated in his pocket as he stood over the kitchen sink finishing off the final third of a granola bar.

The screen said, "Call from Wifey."

"Hey, what's up? Everything good?"

"I've been trying to get ahold of you! Check your texts!"

"Oh, sorry . . . uh . . . yeah, here, one sec . . ."

He opened the text thread and saw the letters, but they didn't register in his mind.

"Get here fast. You're going to be a dad."

"What the—"

He burst into high gear and stuffed anything remotely important into his backpack. He rushed out the front door in a flurry and stumbled back to lock it. He turned on a dime and burst into a full sprint to the car. At eighty-five to ninety miles per hour, he weaved through traffic on the CA-101-north. He floored the old Camry through side streets and yellow lights.

He got the full scoop in the Labor and Delivery room, surrounded by gathering family. The baby's lungs had not developed yet. But his wife's blood pressure was erratic and climbing. They needed to have the baby now.

After the swarm of nurses and doctors in and out of the room, they tried their best at calming conversations. His wife, propped up in the hospital bed, seemed uncharacteristically calm. It was like she was resigned to what awaited. He was still in shock. And before long, the nurses walked in, dressed in paper-like clothes with shower caps and crime scene shoe covers. They said goodbye. As a team effort, the nurses wheeled her away. She would be "put under" for an emergency c-section.

He wondered if he would ever see her again. He hoped that this sudden goodbye would not be their last. The rushed—"I love you, you got this"—was all too brief and passing. The family gathered had left the room. They gave him the time and space to himself. Apart from the company of shock and anxiety, he sat alone. A nurse asked if she could get him anything.

"Uh . . . coffee'd be great?"

He figured the night would be long. The empty room and long hallways felt emptier and longer. The analog clock on the wall tapped in a steady rhythm. He unzipped the backpack with the bare necessities he had rushed to stuff it with. And pulling out a leather-bound Bible, he turned to some pages about a hopeless valley filled with dry bones.

He read the words with his heart more than his eyes.

"Mortal, can these bones live?' I answered, 'O Lord God, you know.'"

But his mind was locked elsewhere. He tried to focus on the words.

"Thus says the Lord God to these bones: I will cause breath to enter you, and you shall live."

But his ears were perked to catch any sound echoing from the hallway. His heart leaped every time a figure passed the open door—but it was just the food cart rumbling, a nurse charting, a doctor making rounds.

Then finally, after an eternity, a nurse walked in. Her face was prime for poker. His heart pinballed in his chest. He held his breath.

Her face turned soft and kind, and she spoke calmly:

"He's a little small . . . but mom and baby are both stable. We're bringing him to the NICU in just a minute."

He exhaled.

A moment later, the Neonatal Intensive Care Unit director showed him how to wash his hands for three minutes and scrub beneath each fingernail with a plastic comb. Then she ushered him into a bright white room where everyone was draped in blues and greens. They wore rubber gloves and wielded shiny tools. Plexiglass isolettes lined both sides of the room. Machines, like arcade games, towered beside each. He stole glances at each clear box, looking for the baby, but the director motioned him to the very end, last on the left. Inside, he saw, for the very first time, his son.

The creature squirmed inside the isolette, like a jellyfish with all his tubes tangling this way and that.

"Go ahead, put your hand on him," the nurse told him, "but with a nice firm touch."

So, he opened one of the plexiglass portals and reached his hand through. He felt his palm completely encircle the baby's rib-cage. He rested his grip on his son like a change-up or a four-seam-fastball. The baby's fists reacted to the touch and swooshed the air. He had grit like a hockey player in his miniature rink. But it was only for a second, and then he let them rest.

The sheet of paper said:

Weight: 3lb 14oz.

Time of birth: 16:53.

Someone asked for his name.

"Ezekiel," his dad said, smiling proudly.

"E-z-e-k-i-e-l?" she repeated as her pencil scratched across the paper.

"Yep. That's it," he beamed.

It wasn't until three or four hours later that he finally saw his wife. She looked pale and tired. Her throat was raw after having been intubated. As the heavy narcotics began to wear off, the gash stapled together across her stomach grew tender with pain. He showed her pictures of the baby. She smiled and closed her eyes.

"Crazy day," she whispered.

Throughout the night and the next few days, he walked the hallways from the Labor and Delivery room to visit the little baby in the NICU. And then, when she was strong enough to be transport-ed, the new mother was wheeled down to see her flesh-and-blood for the first time. She rolled up beside him, and a nurse engaged the wheelchair brakes. As she peeked into his world, a smile split her face. Careful with her own IV tubes, she stretched her arm through the plexiglass window, set her hand upon his chest, and whispered:

"He's so tiny."

The next evening, the NICU doctor knocked on the door as the new mother sifted through a bland dinner. The doctor was quiet and serious but reassured the young couple with a smile. And then she delivered the news. She spoke of a procedure for Ezekiel, one fairly common but challenging, nonetheless, especially on a premature baby. She showed them diagrams on color copy photo paper and said:

"Premature infants have fragile veins. IVs usually last only one to three days. A P.I.C.C. line, though," she continued, "can be used for one to weeks or longer."

"Okay, great . . ." the parents replied, eager for a remedy.

"Well, it *is* difficult—it's a common procedure but can be tricky on a baby of Ezekiel's size."

Her finger pointed to a diagram of a soft plastic tube on the photo paper snaking its way into a central vein. The young parents didn't hesitate to answer.

"Okay, let's do it."

Instead of collapsing veins and needle pokes, they agreed that the P.I.C.C. line was the way to go. It wasn't a difficult decision to make. But anxiety surfaced with it, churning up thoughts for the worst. What if, like with addicts, they can't find the vein? How sure is this? What if all this leads to dire consequences? They hoped against it, though, trusting that all would go smoothly.

It did. A nurse with steady hands pulled off the feat on the first try. She crushed every nerve of their anxiety and silenced their uncertainty. The P.I.C.C. line meant lower exposure to pain and greater stability, but it also set the tone that their stay at the hospital would be a long haul.

Five days after the emergency c-section, the young couple was discharged. The Labor and Delivery ward was full of incoming mothers contracting and families expanding. The postpartum unit had no room to spare. Some said it was thanks to the full moon. They didn't know what to make of it. Their home was only ten miles away, but any distance of separation would mean another obstacle in their path. All they knew was that their baby was still in the NICU, still in the isolette, surviving off machines. Their home had to be here with him.

Fortunately, her parents had a plan. Her dad parked the family travel trailer in the hospital parking lot, and the young couple called it home for the next few weeks. Sam and Margot brought them home-cooked meals along with the mail. Simone dropped off gallons of Starbucks over the weeks. There, they celebrated Valentine's Day with canned soup and dry sandwiches. They watched medivac helicopters from the trailer's window thwapping the air, ambulances screaming by, and frail people in gowns wheeled outside into the sunshine. She pumped every few hours around the clock, and they rejoiced together over a single teaspoon of breast milk. He washed out the parts of the breast pump and tried to say encouraging things. She cried and wanted to hold the baby. Both of them wanted to be home—as a family of three. They wanted it to be easier than it was, but they also didn't know any different.

After a sleepless night in the trailer, the couple walked into the hospital at a slow pace that her post-surgery body could manage. On the way, they spoke of celebrating the "little things" and rejoicing in the small victories. Her milk supply was increasing—from a teaspoon to a tablespoon. The baby wasn't losing weight, and the PICC line was holding for the time being.

After three minutes of scouring their skin to wash away germs, they entered the NICU. Ezekiel's nurse handed the mother a q-tip, and she fed her son for the first time. She dipped the q-tip into her tablespoon of milk and wet his lips. It didn't seem like much, but the nurse said,

"Colostrum is like liquid gold."

Hour after hour, the parents watched their baby breathe with the support of oxygen. The respiratory therapist came by every few hours with his busted nose and kind words. The nurses called him "Mighty Joe." He didn't seem like your typical mixed martial arts fighter, especially considering his gentle touch with the babies.

"I just make a few changes here and there—this dial and that . . ." he told the young dad, "and then God does the rest."

The baby came so early that the young parents missed all their scheduled parenting classes. So, it was trial-by-fire learning how to change dollar bill-sized diapers, bottle feed, and burp the baby. They removed their shirts and held little Ezekiel to their skin like a kangaroo. Even with the wires and tubes tangling, everything in the world felt right. She sang him songs and told him how much she loved him. They bathed him in a plastic box, and his dad read him *The Adventures of Tom Sawyer*. He hoped to be a better dad than Huckleberry Finn's. He prayed his boy would grow up to have courage like Tom.

Despite the circumstances, they normalized the situation as best as they could. They did everything a family might do in their living room. Still, they could not wait to get home. They knew it was a long way away, but they trusted that one day, they'd leave.

One afternoon, like any other, they scrubbed their hands raw in the sink and picked at their fingernails before entering the NICU. The nurses and Mighty Joe, the respiratory therapist, crowded around the isolette at the end, the last plexiglass box on the left. The bells and whistles of machinery sang like an arcade. The nurses stood staring, looking anxious. Ventilators hissed.

Mighty Joe stood beside the baby with his hands in the box. He tapped and pressed the baby's chest rhythmically in synchronization. His eyes darted from the screen to the baby and back again, focused and undaunted. But the baby was blue. The peaks and valleys on the screen plateaued. All the while, the young parents stood still and silent, not quite realizing what was happening. Or perhaps they did, and they figured hoping for the best was the best thing they could do.

The MMA fighter tapped and pressed, eyes going from the screen to the baby and back again. Apparently, this was CPR on a preemie. Beads of sweat percolated on his forehead. The nurses held their breaths. The young couple stood silent with their feet stuck to the tile floor. Then suddenly, the plateau jumped to life, and Ezekiel wailed. His color returned. The room exhaled. A nurse with watery eyes turned to the young couple and gasped,

"You were so calm! Like nothing was happening! You come in, and he's not breathing! Wow!"

The husband said, "Well, uh . . . I guess we didn't really know what was going on."

He did, though. But he figured, somehow, everything would be okay.

It was this resolve that he couldn't escape. Optimism wasn't in his nature. He didn't see the world through rose-colored glasses or even care about glasses being full or empty. It was just in his bones, this knowing confidence. He carried an expectation that what would happen would happen, and somehow, it would be okay. Doubt could slip in like eels, but something beside him and inside him reminded him of some stable certainty.

Some days in the bright white room, it felt crowded and claustrophobic. On others, it was wide and open like a valley. It was rarely quiet, if ever. There was always a solo sung by a fussy baby. The entire NICU choir would sometimes join in, all the babies belting their unique tones together.

Some days were heavy when progress was slow or hard to come by. But these turned into moments when the parents thought to realize how fortunate they were to have a preemie—because it meant extra early time with him.

There was a family with a baby girl born one week before Ezekiel. Her isolette was stationed across from his, and her name was Mirabel. Her four older brothers stood on tiptoes or were held by grandparents to peek through the window to catch glimpses of their baby sister. This family of seven was no stranger to the NICU. They had said goodbye to their fifth son two years before—in the same hospital, same NICU, same station.

As they passed in the hallway, Mirabel's father sparked a conversation, saying:

"Ezekiel, huh? God strengthens."

"Uh. Yeah?" Ezekiel's dad replied.

"Yeah, great name. The meaning, you know?" Mirabel's father said.

"Oh yeah, sure . . . thanks, appreciate it," he replied, remembering that he had read that somewhere.

In the travel trailer, between spoonfuls of canned soup, he reran the conversation with Mirabel's father in his mind. I can't imagine what they're going through. He thought to himself—*Who is this guy? And how in the world can he do what he is doing?*

Perhaps it was a question that others thought of them. How did they manage to do what they were doing?

Another conversation with the NICU doctor. She used fancy words to describe how Ezekiel was born with a hole in his heart.

"In a nutshell," the doctor said, "it's affecting his lungs and heart, the flow of blood and oxygen."

Their own lungs grew heavy with worry.

"We're going to schedule an echocardiogram to take a closer look."

"Uh . . . oh . . . okay."

Later in the day, a specialist wheeled in a machine the size of a fridge. He squirted a gooey substance on Ezekiel's chest and moved a device across his tiny frame. His heart shone in black and white on the screen, like a boa constrictor coiled up and pulsing. The specialist clicked on a mouse and recorded the *woosh-woosh-woosh* of the baby's heartbeat. He took measurements and turned dials and knobs. The parents prayed. They prayed specifically—

"This heart . . . it belongs to you, Jesus."

After the exam, it was determined that the hole, somehow, was gone. The hole in the baby's heart had closed. It didn't make sense.

Days and weeks passed, and Ezekiel's weight steadily climbed. The doctor slowly weaned him off oxygen, ridding him of one less attachment to the machines. But between gulps of milk or in moments of stillness, the six-week-old would forget to breathe. His heart rate would drop, and alarms would send nurses rushing over.

The nurses and doctors reassured the parents that the baby's lungs weren't fully developed yet. So, they began to see it as merely another hurdle—not insurmountable, but just another mountain to climb. When his heart rate would plummet, and the machines would alarm to the key of B-flat, the parents learned to gather their nerves, tickle his toes, or run their fingers along his back. It's what they saw the nurses do. So, in time, each of them grew in their confidence and even their expectation of what was happening.

However, the days and weeks grew long. Moving home out of the travel trailer put distance between the new parents and the baby. They'd call in late at night and first thing in the morning for updates. And sure enough, the baby had had another episode. It was an unending cycle, it seemed.

The doctor ordered a twenty-four-hour brain scan to check for seizures. Another occasion for anxiety. Or simply another hurdle to climb. They prayed as a specialist stretched a wire netting with probes across his skull. They asked others to pray. Their family prayed. Friends prayed. Mirabel's parents prayed. Nurses prayed.

They knew full well that things could go south. But something was pressing them to trust. It kept them believing and confident, even when the reasons weren't quite there. So, they prayed.

The machines indicated no issues with seizures. Nothing gave the impression of abnormal brain activity. But they still couldn't figure out why the baby would stop breathing. The reason for his dropping heart rate remained a mystery. The doctor spoke of consulting more specialists to better coordinate Ezekiel's breathing and eating. But it didn't explain why the episodes happened during his sleep.

The parents continued to tread water. Some days they felt like going home was a far-off fantasy. On others, it felt closer than ever. And then, on some, they tried not to think of it. Tissue boxes emptied, and words, sometimes, ran short. They grew weary and didn't say the right things at the right times, or they said the right things at the wrong times.

The parents watched as one baby after another was discharged. Some had journeyed long with Ezekiel, others only a few short days. Even Mirabel went home while they continued to search for answers. *Envy* wasn't the correct term for what they felt. It was more *bittersweet.* It was joyous and precisely what they wanted for Mirabel and for themselves. Instead of sulking into despair, they learned to strengthen their resolve, shaping their lives around the knowing that this was a season. This was a period of waiting for what would come.

When Ezekiel reached two months of age, a nurse posed the question of anemia. She wondered whether putting the baby back on oxygen might help keep him alert. The doctor called for a blood draw, and after squeezing ruby droplets from the baby's heel, it was determined his iron level was low.

On oxygen, Ezekiel came to life. He perked up and suckled without his heart stopping. He slept and didn't stop breathing. For six days, the baby managed to keep it up. And on the deciding factor of the seventh day, he did too.

And now, after the baby was fit for an at-home heart monitor and a mobile oxygen canister, he has just passed his final test. He kept his lungs breathing and his heart beating for a full ninety minutes while strapped into a car seat. It is the last hurdle before the hurdle of everything awaiting.

As they set out from the only home the baby's known, there is a heaviness mixed with joy. It's like the emotional toll of everything crashes upon the room. The parents sob like babies—overcome with gratitude and terrifying uncertainty ahead. They wipe their eyes and noses repeatedly, but the faucets still run. Their hearts are two sizes too full. There are no words to adequately express thanks.

After nine long weeks—sixty-three days, to be exact—the family of three takes their first step outside the NICU doors. They're all smiles and tears.

Ezekiel feels the sunshine on his skin for the first time. He smells the exhaust of cars crawling south on the 101. He hears birds chirp and sees the blue of the sky. For the first time, he sleeps in his own bed, a rickety bassinet that's held every baby in the family since 1956. For the first time, he is home, just like they hoped he would.

8

Splagchnizomai

THEY HAD BEEN MISSING since Tuesday.

The family of four drove off in the Volkswagen, leaving grandma and grandpa waving in the rearview mirror. The police say a MasterCard was used at the Mobil station in Sutherlin and a cell tower pinged their way through Wolf Creek.

But that was Tuesday.

Behind the booth of community shoes and anti-fungal spray, Cedric stares at the news ticker. It's a commercial break, but the CNN news reports keep churning out details of their top story. Sofia's birthday party lined up for slick-soled shoes waits impatiently as Cedric turns up the volume on the TV. The news anchors return with more details emerging.

"Family of four headed for the California coast goes missing in the Wild Rogue Wilderness, a remote area of southwestern Oregon."

Sofia, the one with the crown, motions for her mom to come over.

"With heavy snow and high elevation, John, the situation is turning grim."

"It is heartbreaking, Erica, especially with two young daughters."

Sofia's mom taps the counter, jolting Cedric back to life.

"Uh . . . could we get some help here? These girls are ready to bowl. We have lanes seven and eight 'til 3pm," Sophia's mother snaps.

"Of . . . of course."

As Cedric sets out rental shoes, he keeps his ears perked for any sound-byte offering new developments. He steals a glance at the TV between partygoers asking for size threes and fours. Then, after the eternal procession of Sofia's birthday party and a smile to a smile-less mother, he returns his full attention to CNN's top story. Sure enough, it's a commercial break.

Cedric's been following the story since Tuesday. The family of four never made it home after a weekend with the grandparents. Of course, people go missing every day, but this, for some reason, felt different. Maybe it's the kids—stuck somewhere—who knows where—in the mountains with all that snow.

Since Tuesday, he had been glued to the screen. Between the splatter of pins and drops of bowling balls, he heard the breaking news of Kevin Lee, a computer programmer, his wife Annie, and their two kids, Brynn, age four, and Maggie, seven months old. They've been missing for six days now. Cedric feared their chances of survival dropped by the hour. It was something he felt in his gut more than in his head.

They had interviewed the grandparents and friends, who pleaded through tears for anyone with information to come forward. Video montages showed bloodhounds, snowmobiles, and helicopters searching the vast forests and treacherous slopes. Cedric even wondered how he might join the search. But he's two thousand miles away, and his shift isn't up until 8pm.

It didn't keep him from longing to help. With each passing day, Cedric felt the urge to cut ties and go. The thought was crazy, though. Who in their right mind would drive across the country for some strangers? He figures, though, people do crazy things all the time. The news always talked about people spending days in line for the newest video game system or traveling hours for big waves and perfect skiing conditions.

Cedric shivers off the cold and enters his cramped apartment. He snatches the remote from the faded couch and brings the TV to life. A lot may have changed between locking up the bowling alley and his walk four blocks home. He stands before the screen, ice melting from his boots into the carpet.

"Data logs of cell sites are directing the search to the western region . . ."

This was something new. A section of the map on the screen is highlighted in red. And while it looks narrow, the digital image hardly can account for the rough terrain, steep slopes, and thick timber.

A survival expert speaks of keeping warm and hydrated. He assesses how the Lee family could prolong their survival if they limit their exertion and ration whatever leftovers they might have. Cedric feels guilt inside as he reheats a chicken pot pie.

He spent the next three nights falling asleep on the couch to CNN Tonight. Two mornings had left him with little in the way of new developments, just more footage of search-and-rescue hikers and improved digital maps. But on the third day, he's awakened to the big red letters: "BREAKING NEWS."

The ticker reads: *"Local helicopter pilot spots mother and daughters."*

Cedric triples the volume and stands up from the couch. The news anchor relays the development:

"A local helicopter pilot spotted Mrs. Lee and her two daughters along a remote road."

Cedric shifts on his feet.

"They were walking through the snow . . ."

"Oh, thank God!" Cedric blurts out to the empty apartment.

"Thank God," he exhales.

He holds his breath for more.

"What of the dad? Kevin Lee? What of him?" he says to himself.

The anchor continues:

"Mrs. Lee and her daughters were airlifted out of the area and transferred to a nearby hospital."

"But what of the husband? What of Kevin?!" Cedric says aloud.

"Authorities are combing the area for any sign of Mr. Kevin Lee. We'll have more still to come as the story unfolds."

Commercial break.

A broken Icee machine and a malfunction on lane two peel Cedric away from the news throughout the day. But rushing back, he learns that the Lees had taken a wrong turn and ended up some twenty-three miles down a remote road. It's there in a snowy ravine where their Volkswagen got stuck. Annie didn't speak to reporters, but according to the sheriff conducting the press release, the Lees had run the car's engine to keep warm. As the snow blanketed the vehicle and they ran out of gas, they used magazines and dried wood for a campfire. Sometime later, Mr. Lee burned the tires of the Volkswagen in hopes of signaling rescuers.

At the press conference, there's the snap and flash from high-dollar cameras. The sheriff commits all the resources of the multi-coordinated departments to locate and bring Mr. Kevin Lee home safe and sound.

Cedric feels the elation bubbling in his chest. He embraces the act of rising to the occasion, feeling motivated for the challenge ahead. But Cedric's two thousand miles away. It's not like he could possibly help. But what of all the celebrities chasing natural disasters? God bless 'em. Either they're in it for the publicity, or their hearts are moved to join in with relief efforts. But he's no celebrity. It's outrageous that he should even think of going—he's a bowling alley manager in the upper-Midwest living paycheck to paycheck. It's crazy. Still, hope and longing mix inside of him. And there's the ache for Annie, her girls, and the unknown whereabouts of the rock in their lives.

He's not sure why, but Cedric can't let it go. These are strangers across the country. They've never crossed paths. They have no mutual acquaintances. If they passed one another at the deli or a shopping mall, they wouldn't know any different. Who knows if they'd even get along?

But for Cedric, somehow, it's all beside the point. He's never been married. He's never had a kid. His sister has a son, but they're in Memphis, and the rest of his blood relatives are spread across— from sea to shining sea. So, his day-to-day family is composed mainly of the patrons at Harley's Bowl and church choir members.

CNN's ongoing coverage of the Lees makes the world feel a lot smaller for Cedric. His connection with the Lees has become personal—intimate almost. But it's also shifted how Cedric sees those closest to him—at the bowling alley and church. He's noticed a softening in his tone, a new patience to his haste. The fuse shortened by his usual irritation seems to be lengthening. At choir practice, he feels himself pause, and with moist eyes, he looks over the group with new affection. He appreciates the members who are like a family to him—Ms. Simmons and her famous peanut butter cookies or those who invited him over for holidays and dropped off soup when he was sick. He feels a profound sense of giving back. They are like his own.

He's starting to feel for the Lees as if they are his own. Sure, they might be faces on the TV, but couldn't that be anybody? His sister and nephew in Memphis? Any one of the choir members? He feels moved inside, moved actually to move—to do something. But what?

He thought about writing them—the mom and the girls. And so, after his shift, he scribbles out words across a notepad. He sits on the couch, still in his coat and boots, but he doesn't know how to start.

"*Dear Annie and Brynn and Maggie*" sounds too personal, like they went to high school or played in the band together. But "*Dear Mrs. Lee and family*" sounds too formal. And he's not sure what to say after.

That his heart was breaking for these complete strangers?
That his insides were churning, and he couldn't sleep?
That he suffered over their situation?

He rips the paper from the pad, crumples it, and tosses it aside.

Later that night, he finds a Go Fund Me page where he contributes enough to make him overdraft. But that hardly helps when your husband or dad is lost in the snow.

Cedric must do something, but he needs to figure out what. Sending "thoughts and prayers" feels like next to nothing, even though his pastor says, "prayer is the most powerful thing you can do." His bank account's feeling the pinch after the Go Fund Me deposit, but it's hardly comparable to what the Lees are going through.

He remembers Sean Penn and Wyclef Jean helping in the rubble of Haiti, Steve Buscemi on 9/11 spending days pulling out bodies from Ground Zero. They did something more than Cedric. More than just "thoughts and prayers."

On the television, he sees the phone number asking anyone with information to come forward. Almost impulsively, he dials the eight hundred number.

"Hi, thank you for calling the Kevin Lee Missing Person Hotline," says a kind voice, eager with anticipation.

"Uh, hi," Cedric breathes.

"Yes, how can I help you, sir? Do you have any information pertinent to locating Mr. Kevin Lee?" she asks.

"Um, no . . . no. But um . . . I'd really like to help. And I'm not sure how?"

"Okay, great, thank you," she says on the other end of the line.

"If you're in adequate shape, we've got volunteer search parties gathering each morning at 8am at the Boys and Girls Club on Rocklin and Second Street here in Wilderville."

She assumes he's local or at least regional and offering his services. Without telling her that he's two thousand miles away, Cedric scribbles down the address and says,

"Thanks much, ma'am. Appreciate it."

"Well, thank you, sir! We appreciate your support!"

The news details further developments of how Kevin Lee set out from his family on Wednesday to seek help. He had on a navy-blue jacket, sneakers, and jeans. After Kevin studied a map, Annie said her husband believed the nearest town was about four or five miles away. He promised her he'd return that same day if he couldn't find anyone. But he never returned.

Cedric phones his boss. He's committed now, even though it sounds crazy.

"Cedric?!" says a scratchy voice, groggy with sleep.

"Hi, boss," Cedric says.

"Do you have any idea what time it is?!"

"Uh . . . yeah, sorry for calling so late. The thing is, I'm calling to see about taking tomorrow off?"

"Really?! 11:45pm—it's nearly tomorrow already!"

Cedric's silent on the other end of the phone.

His boss calms and collects himself. With a change of tone, he sighs and asks,

"What's going on, Cedric?"

"Well, you see, I know this is gonna sound kinda crazy, but . . ."

Cedric recounts the last ten days and his need to drive out to help the Lees. Everything within him is screaming to help. His boss listens in silence and then replies:

"I'm sorry, Cedric, it's just not possible."

Cedric's heart drops. His frustration boils. His mind shifts to whether he should quit, right here on the spot, over the phone. He's probably not thinking straight. But the emotions get the better of him, and he blurts out:

"Okay then, well, if that's the case—"

"But tell you what—" his boss interrupts, "sounds crazy, but if you gotta go, you gotta go. Work a half-day, and then you're good to go. I'll even pitch in for the gas."

Cedric leaves work at noon and floors the pedal of his Pontiac Grand Prix. The car speeds across snowy fields, a tundra of white. Flying might make more sense, but the nearest airport is hours away and it would cost a fortune. So, Cedric exerts the engine of the Pontiac, knowing full well that Mr. Lee's survival chances continue to drop by the hour. He gasses up in Fargo and stretches his legs long enough to purchase a rotisserie hot dog and black coffee. As he blows the steam from the cup, he still can't quite believe he's on his way. It all sounds crazy. But everything in him is moving Cedric to help. After Fargo, he doesn't stop across an inch of North Dakota.

Cedric uses a filthy truck stop bathroom in Montana and refuels on caffeine. His foot feels cramped from pressing the accelerator. He keeps awake through the night with the windows cracked and the sound of the radio blaring. Between the icy chill and the obstructed silence, he keeps his eyes open.

He pictures Kevin Lee shivering somewhere in the cold. He figures Annie and the girls must be in a hospital room with bandages across frostbitten toes and their arms stuck full of IVs. His ordeal pales in comparison. There is no comparison. Kevin Lee's a perfect stranger, but he's a husband and a dad. And just being somebody, anybody—isn't that enough?

To his left, he passes Bozeman. The "most livable city" is asleep. He drives along the I-90 without a taste of its Montana livability. The sun also rises as he leaves Montana, and just outside Boise, the news sent through the speakers of his Pontiac has him pulling off the highway and slamming the shifter into park.

"Kevin Lee's body was found today after a massive search."

9

Aphiemi

SHE'S NOT SURE IF she could ever forget. But she's confident she will never forgive.

The ghost of where her father stood still reeks of booze. But he's long gone. After another brawl in the living room—the kind that leaves the lamps upended and shards of porcelain plates across the carpet—he said he wouldn't be coming back.

He said all sorts of things—words that leave cuts so deep they misshapen your skin. Stitches won't do. Surgery is useless. Whether it's truth or emotion or inebriation, the truth is his words and fists dealt a death blow to their family.

He threw t-shirts in a gym bag and cleared his clothing from the drawers. He ransacked the coffee can for dollar bills and emptied his children's piggybanks of every coin. He stormed through the house, thunder rumbling with each footstep.

She usually claimed the bathroom when he would get like this. There's a lock on the door, and even as hard as he pounded, he hadn't busted it yet. He could, she's sure of it, but for some reason, he had yet to splinter the door. She'd lie in the tub with her hands cupped over her ears, waiting out the screams and shattering of things.

When the police showed up, it would only make matters worse. Jail time only intensified the issue. Sophia's father would always return—always worse off than before—more calloused. But this evening, it feels like his boomerang days were through.

Sophia had unlocked the bathroom door and ventured into the chaos. Shouts and screams reverberated across the small square footage of the place. Everything rumbled. Framed family pictures fell from their hooks and shattered across the floor. His hands pounded the cabinets, the drywall, and her mother. The living room was an earthquake.

"I swear to God, Rosa!"

"What are you talking about?!"

"Dammit! WHAT DO YOU WANT ME TO DO?!" he screamed.

"I don't know—I don't know—I don't know. I'm sorry! I'm sorr—!" Rosa sobbed.

"—Forget it! I'm done. DONE. I'm sick of all your shi—"

"—NO! Please don't. Don't go, Steve! Steve, I'm begging you!"

Sophia watched in horror at the unraveling of her family. Her father stood menacing above while her mother collapsed at his feet. Most times, he'd cool off and come to his senses. But he never threatened to leave. Ever. Until now.

Her mother pleaded with him to stay.

"Please, please, PLEASE!" she screamed.

How strange it was to ask him to stay. Especially as the bruises around her mother's throat began to darken.

"Please, don't go! No! Please, PLEASE—I'm begging you."

But his face was a statue, his eyes ablaze. He threw on his coat and swiped the keys from the counter. He shifted the gym bag higher up his shoulder. The kid's coins jingled in the side pocket.

He made his way to the door and then stopped. He glanced back. It was either a moment of clarity or a final goodbye—one last look to burn into his memory. His eyes scanned the room, moist and searching. Perhaps he looked back on all the wreckage? Maybe his eyes saw the memories of better times—before the stress, the drink, the fighting. His eyes met the brown of his daughter's. She stared back, her cheeks slick with tears, but her mouth couldn't form a word.

There were thousands of things she wished she could say. But her lips wouldn't let her. They quivered wordlessly. The disconnect between her brain and voice was a grand canyon. And without a word from anyone, her father slammed the door behind him.

Sophia's mother sits on the kitchen floor with her back against the wall. She clutches her head in her hands, sobbing. The tears tap like rain on the linoleum. In the adjacent room, her little brother hides beneath the covers. He squeezes the life out of a stuffed kangaroo—and shakes. Sophia's insides feel cavernous as she stands in the wasteland of the apartment. Outside the window, she can hear the roar of an engine as her father leaves the family.

She's not sure how long she's been waiting by the window. She stares out, looking for any sign of the old truck returning. Her ears are peeled for a knock at the door or the sound of a key undoing the lock.

She pictures her father rushing in with tears, hugs, and "I'm sorry" on his lips. He would return a new man—transformed in every way. He wouldn't reek of booze but fine cologne. Or, at the very least, he'd smell like hard work—oil and dirt. He'd interlace his dirty fingers with her small smooth ones. And as he would dance with her in the living room, he'd steal a kiss from her mother and tussle her brother's hair.

But the hours grow long, and so do the days. No roar of the truck returning. No knock at the door or key in the lock. There's no phone call. There's nothing—just a gaping hole in Sophia's heart and an empty space at the table.

Three days pass before they manage to right the wreck of their apartment. They sweep the glass carefully, tossing the busted picture frames into the dumpster. Nothing is back to normal. Everything has changed. But the apartment is somewhat the same—just fewer plates and bent light fixtures.

Sophia's mom wears dark sunglasses and a scarf to get groceries. It's the middle of winter, so a scarf isn't out of the ordinary. But sunglasses in snowy overcast turns some heads. Bruising would turn more, though.

At school, Sophia can't concentrate. Everything surges forward while she's stuck in place. She feels left behind by long division. The splitting of numbers just adds to the frustration. In class, they learn about Abraham Lincoln. But all she can wonder is why he stayed when everything was falling apart.

As the days turn into weeks, there's still no knock at the door or key in the lock. There's no phone call. There's nothing. Bitterness begins to take root in Sophia's heart. It's the type of seed that grows even in a Minnesota winter.

"I hate you, daddy!" she screams into her pillow.

"I hate you! I hate you! I hate you!"

Sophia grows crabby in her tone to her mother and brother—lashing out new choice words with spite. Her skin is thin on the receiving end of things as she bursts into tears and rushes to her room. And with her tears, she soaks her mattress.

Insecurity gorges on her unanswered questions and starves every ounce of her self-worth. She's not sure why her father left. She's even less sure why he hasn't returned. What is it about her that made him go? What did she do to lose his love?

Sophia searches for his old truck on the way to school, looking out both sides of the bus windows. But it's never any luck. She tries calling from the landline at home or the payphone by the drugstore. Each time she dials, she holds her breath. And between the rings, she clings to hope—until the line disconnects.

On a frigid afternoon, Ms. Simmons stops Sophia in the mail room. She lives in the apartment below Sophia and what's left of her family. And while the mailroom is the way out of the building, Ms. Simmons never goes out anymore. She grips a stack full of mail in one hand, and in the other, she drags along an oxygen tank.

"What's wrong, dear?" Ms. Simmons asks, her eyes concerned and searching.

"Uh . . . no-nothing," says Sophia, faking a smile.

"Honey, it's okay if you wanna talk," Ms. Simmons offers.

"Oh, I'm good, thank you," lies Sophia.

"Okay, sweetheart. Just know that I'm always here—apartment number twenty-seven—if you wanna talk. Anytime, I mean it. I've got the time. Or we could just play board games? I've got checkers and cards and Monopoly somewhere, too."

"Thank-thank you, ma'am," Sophia says as she rushes up the stairs.

As she closes the door to the apartment, Sophia thinks of everything she'd like to tell Ms. Simmons—all the thousands of things she wishes she could say. But to talk about it feels like a betrayal.

What does Ms. Simmons know about her anyway? She can't possibly understand what's going on. No. It's too personal. It's secret.

Sophia opens the fridge, her stomach aching for anything edible. School lunch is mostly all she can count on nowadays. But Sophia finds a bag of bread with one last dried-up heel. As she spreads out the last bit of jam on the bread, she hears a knock at the door.

She drops the knife and empty jar of jam and sprints to the door. Her heart nearly leaps through her chest. With her ear to the door, she cries out, just like her mother taught her:

"Who is it?"

But in her excitement, she can't make out the voice through the door. Her heart beats so fast it keeps her from hearing.

"Who is it?!" she cries again.

"It's . . . " comes the mumble through the door.

She still can't hear who it is, so she asks again, "Hello? Who is it?"

"It's Marsha . . . uh . . . Ms. Simmons from down below."

Sophia's heart sinks. As she opens the door, her face betrays her.

"Aw, I'm sorry, sweetheart," says Ms. Simmons through labored breaths.

It's like she's a mind reader.

Ms. Simmons continues breathlessly, "I just thought I'd drop this off if that's okay?"

She holds a plate stacked with peanut butter cookies. The cookies fog up the saran wrap and fill the hallway with a sweet, nutty smell. Sophia's eyes grow wide. Her letdown transforms into something a little less. Then it hits her—the embarrassment—as she realizes that Ms. Simmons had climbed an entire flight of stairs to deliver it.

"Uh, thank you, Ms. Simmons," Sophia smiles shyly as she takes the plate, "so kind of you."

"Ah, it's nothing. Here, I brought you this too."

Beneath the plate was a magazine—National Geographic.

"Thought you might like it," Ms. Simmons says, pointing to the magazine, "there's some really great stuff in there."

Sophia shifts the plate of cookies to one hand and takes the magazine in the other. On the cover is a picture of a panda and words about efforts to save them. Sophia looks up as Ms. Simmons wheels away her oxygen and calls after her, "Thank you!"

"Of course," Ms. Simmons waves back.

For the next hour and a half, Sophia drops cookie crumbs across the pages of a magazine that stinks of coffee and cigarettes. Most of the pages are warped where a spill has dried, but she couldn't care less. The pictures take her away from a bitter Minnesota winter. The stories move her mind off the hole in her heart. For a moment, she's not a girl with a daddy who doesn't want her.

Then she flips to a dogeared page titled "Astonishing Stories From Rwanda."

Jean Ngenzi has a warm smile, and his friends call him quiet and kind. But after he lost everything and everyone in the genocide of '94, he was seething in rage. Bitterness replaced the warm smile. He only wanted revenge.

"The Hutus shot my father in the church. They riddled his body with bullets. They cut my mother with a machete, and she bled out in the hills. So did my brother and two sisters. My whole family was murdered."

"I said, 'When I grow up, I want to be a soldier, so I can kill them all.'"

Jean made a list of all the people he planned to kill. They were neighbors, shopkeepers, teachers, and other Hutus from the community.

But after July 1994, with the help of trauma counseling, Jean slowly processed the genocide and what it meant for him. Unbelievably,

Jean took steps toward forgiveness. The steps were slow and painful, but he burned the list of those he wanted to kill. Instead, he chose to forgive.

Jean says, "I learned it's not 'forgive and forget.' There's no such thing. I forgive, but I cannot forget. Because forgetting means not forgiving. No, I remember. And in remembering, I choose to live differently—in forgiveness. It doesn't mean no justice. I know full well what my once-enemies did. They should be tried, prosecuted, and brought to justice. But now I learn to call them my friends."

Now, almost thirty years later, Jean is a Child Protection Officer in Rwanda. He hires Hutus—his once-sworn enemies—to work for him. Jean even married one. As a Child Protection Officer, Jean makes every day an opportunity to extend love to the people he once hated. He hopes to make Rwanda famous for forgiveness.

When Colette Gasana was ten, the genocide against the Tutsi people began. Colette witnessed what no child ever should.

"Hutus murdered us Tutsis. But Hutus were our friends. They didn't come from other countries or far away—they were our neighbors."

Colette hid in the bushes with her sister when she heard the mob in their neighborhood. Through the leaves, she watched as her Hutu neighbors tortured, mutilated, and murdered her mother and father. Colette also saw the murder of her aunts and uncles. Her grandmother was beaten and left for dead, but she didn't die. To this day, she has a mental disability due to brain damage and trauma.

When the genocide ended, Colette was lost, unable to move on. Christian organizations tried gathering children, but it wasn't easy. So many were gone, and those left were scared. Others were children of perpetrators. Colette never imagined she could stand the sight of those who stole her family from her. But along the way, she learned a profound lesson about forgiveness.

"I learned Love," she said.

"Love. Love. Love. It's a word taught every time in the program."

Colette shares how the Christian message of Jesus's sacrifice helps her forgive those who murdered her family.

"God forgave me. So, I must forgive. That's the bottom line."

But her forgiveness went beyond words and into action.

Colette made it her mission to care for poor and orphaned children in Rwanda. Through her organization "Rwanda Kids," Colette has made a conscious effort to help both Tutsi and Hutu children—by sponsoring them with food, clothing, medical aid, and schooling.

She said, "Most of the children are Hutu. They come from families who committed genocide. If I can't forgive them, who can I forgive? If I can't help them, who can I help? Only Tutsis? No. I couldn't do that. But then there was this boy whose father was in the gang that killed my parents. They were our neighbors. After the bloodshed, the father went to jail for his crime. So, when there were children to help, I said, 'Bring his child. The boy needs a family.'"

Sophia wipes the page not of crumbs but of her tears.

"I'm so glad you finally came," says Ms. Simmons as she moves a red checker diagonally to an empty black square.

"Thanks for the cookies the other day, Ms. Simmons," Sophia replies.

"Oh dear, just call me Marsha—your turn."

"Okay," Sophia smiles as she double-jumps Marsha's two red checkers.

"Hey, now!" Marsha exclaims.

"Sorry about that," Sophia suddenly clams up.

"Oh, I'm only teasing, dear," Marsha smiles, "it's okay!"

Sophia's icy stiffness quickly melts away as Marsha offers her a cup of hot cocoa.

"I'm just glad you came by," says Marsha, "it sure gets lonely down here."

"Are you by yourself *all day*?" asks Sophia.

"Yep. Except when my son comes by. He's a basketball coach. Do you play?"

"Um . . . not really," Sophia moves a black checker to an empty square.

"How about dancing or drawing?"

"I like to read," Sophia says, eyes studying the board.

"Me too!" says Marsha, jumping a red checker over the one Sophia just placed.

"How'd you like the magazine I dropped off?" Marsha asks.

Sophia looks up and says, "I liked the pictures of the pandas and the stuff about the sharks. I'd be scared to swim in the ocean, though."

"Yeah, me too," smiles Marsha.

"And . . . " Sophia pauses, "there was that stuff about Africa in there."

"Rwanda?"

"Yeah," says Sophia, eyes darting back to the board.

"Hmm," says Marsha, feigning interest in her next move on the checkerboard. And then, throwing caution to the wind, she says,

"You know, um . . . my daddy wasn't really there for us . . . I remember crying my eyes out when he'd come home. Like the devil got a hold of him. He was angry and mean and rotten—with his words and . . . sometimes . . . even with his fists."

Marsha sips her coffee. Sophia sits up, uncertain.

"I remember he smelled like the sewer and looked like a wild man."

"What'd you do?" asks Sophia.

"Hid. Cried," Marsha sighs, "and I remember one time when he got especially mean and nasty, I told him to—well . . . I don't think your mama would want me teaching you those words," Marsha laughs solemnly.

She continues, "But somewhere along the way, I learned that sadly, daddy ain't gonna change. That was a hard lesson to learn. Sad but true. I could be madder than a wet hen, but that wasn't gonna change nothing."

Marsha readjusts her nasal cannula before continuing,

"I don't know if it was the war or the drink, but he was always in a rage. And I'd fight back, talk back, spit back, cry, run, hide, blame—but nothing *ever* changed."

"So," Marsha says, "I figured forgiveness was just about the last thing I could do."

"But did he deserve it?" asks Sophia.

"It's complicated," Marsha says. "What he was doing was wrong. No excuse for that. Just plain wrong. He was no daddy to us, no husband to my mama. He deserved to go to jail. And he did. But jail didn't solve the problem."

Sophia looks up at Marsha, meeting her eyes momentarily.

"But I learned, later on, that God knows. And God sees everything. God doesn't turn a blind eye to nothing. That gave me some hope."

Sophia studies Marsha's face.

"Even still, I carried all this weight—I grew angry and sad inside—because of him. But one day, it all got too heavy, and I had to try to forgive—not just for him, but for me."

Marsha clears her throat, hydrating the dryness brought on by the oxygen before continuing,

"Forgiveness is complicated. It's a process, you know? Everyday. But it ain't about letting him off the hook for what he did. But it does mean freeing myself from all that."

Marsha reflects quietly for a moment and then says,

"I don't know. Maybe it means giving that hook to God, letting God decide what to do with it. I finally learned after all these years—forgiveness is about my attitude, not his action."

Sophia stares.

"It ain't right what your daddy's doing, sweetheart," Marsha dares, "it's wrong through and through. But I'm here for you. No matter what, sweetheart. Protect you, support you, listen to you, whatever you need."

Sophia wipes her eyes.

"And this forgiveness . . . don't mean you have to be in a relationship with him. He gave up that right. Sure, he'll always be your daddy, and maybe things'll change someday."

Marsha slides her the box of tissues.

"But for you, right now, know this—you are a *strong young lady*," Marsha emphasizes each word.

Sophia sniffs.

"We're gonna get through this. Might take a lot of cookies and checkers, but one day, Sophia, we will."

10

Shalom

THE OLD CHEVY CATCHES its breath in the falling snow. It idles and exhausts as snowflakes drop in lines around it. The passenger door screeches open—the sound of bending metal from an indented side panel.

"Sorry to keep you waiting, Mike," says Jimmy.

He leaps into the cab and slams the door shut.

"Not a worry. Just about everything slows in this sort of snow."

"Yep. Goes with the territory," says Jimmy.

"So, where we off to?" asks Mike.

"Yeah, I really appreciate you doing this, Mike. You know my Uncle Charlie's? He's out past the interstate—I figure we head out there first and take a look. Maybe double back for what we need?"

"Sure thing," replies Mike, "I know the place."

The tires of the old Chevy press new treads in the fresh snow as the engine throttles up. It's about a ten-minute drive to the farm where Uncle Charlie keeps his tractors. The soil won't thaw for a few months, but Uncle Charlie keeps his tractors running through the winter in case he needs one to double as a plow.

"How's Olivia doing? And the kids?" asks Mike as he pulls through the intersection.

"Kids are great—and Olivia? She's hanging tough," says Jimmy.

"Oh yeah?" asks Mike.

"Yeah, she's a trooper."

Mike lets the silence settle in and form between them. Between the hum of the engine and the tires mashing the snow, Jimmy continues,

"Yeah, but it's been tough to tell you the truth."

"Yeah?" asks Mike.

"Guess it goes with the territory—three kids and all. And the job, it's a grind. Most days, we're barely keeping our heads above water. And we're swimming so hard," Jimmy confesses as he stares out the window.

"Hmm."

"Sounds silly," Jimmy scoffs, "it's one thing to have something awful happen—cancer, or a stroke or something. And, I feel bad for even saying it—but we're struggling, Mike."

"Oh yeah?" Mike looks over.

"I mean, we're healthy. Kids are good. Sure, there's the marital squabbles, but that's normal, right? And yeah, issues at work—but it's like . . . I just feel gassed, you know? Empty."

"What seems to be the problem?" asks Mike.

"Not sure exactly. Just not firing on all cylinders, I guess."

"You sleep all right?" asks Mike.

"Guess so?"

"Money problems?" Mike continues.

"Not more than anyone," replies Jimmy.

"Just feel like the fire's gone? Locked on cruise control?" asks Mike.

"Sounds about right," says Jimmy.

"Hmm."

"Feels like I'm just plodding along, trapped in routine. Maybe it's a luxury some folks can't afford, but . . . don't know where I'm headed."

"Yeah?" says Mike.

"Doldrums of life, I guess. Like that one movie where every day's the same—bleeds into the next—"

"—Groundhog Day," says Mike.

"Yeah, that's it. Same old thing. Goes with the territory, I guess," Jimmy sighs.

Mike takes the road past the outskirts of town along a barbed wire fence that separates the road from a field beneath the snow.

"Can I give you some advice?" Mike asks.

"Gladly," Jimmy replies.

"Think about what brings you joy. Make a gratitude list. Ten things you're grateful for. It's what we do in A.A., especially when we can't see straight. Try it."

"Okay, yeah, sure."

Jimmy sits silent and looks out at empty trees across the snowy landscape. The wipers push heavy flakes across the windshield. After a minute, Mike's voice cuts through the silence,

"I mean, right now."

"Oh, okay," says Jimmy, caught unawares.

"Number one, top of the list," says Mike, "what is it? 'I'm grateful for . . .?'"

"Oh, uh . . . Oliva and the kids, of course. Grateful for them."

"That's two. So, how about number three?"

"Umm . . . job, house, friends."

"So that's halfway—five more to go. Think on it," says Mike as he pulls off the highway onto a snowy farm road. At the end of the stretch, the truck slows up before a big barn with red paint peeling along the grooves in the wood.

Mike yanks the gearshift into park and turns to Jimmy,

"Think on it," he repeats, "and find out what's missing."

The keys in the ignition force a chiming sound as Mike and Jimmy open the doors and hop out of the cab.

Inside the barn, bright bulbs hang from the rafters and shine on a ruby-red tractor. It's the iconic 1941 Farmall Model A with rear tires as tall as Christmas trees. The tractor has a pan seat and a high-extended steering wheel. At 16.32 horsepower, it's best known for pushing through rows of wheat and soybeans. But when the snow's heavy and Uncle Charlie's in a pinch, it doubles just fine as a plow.

"Engine won't turn over," grunts Uncle Charlie as he wipes the grease off his hands.

"Yeah?" says Mike.

"Appreciate you coming by."

"Sure thing," says Mike, "Jimmy mentioned you needed a hand. You check the spark plugs?"

"Yes, sir."

"How 'bout the wires?"

"No issues there," answers Uncle Charlie.

"You put gas in it?"

Uncle Charlie laughs, "C'mon, Mike."

"I trust you," Mike smiles, "let's take a look. Might have something to do with the fuel system."

Around town, Mike's known for having "a tool for every trouble," and his expertise at the hardware store is not limited to construction. He dabbles in machinery. But when you've lived as long as Mike in the Midwest, chances are, you know something about tractors. Uncle Charlie certainly knows more, but he's past his prime. He could probably diagnose the problem, but in his old age, he enjoys the camaraderie of his nephew Jimmy and his old pal Mike.

Jimmy stands beside Mike and the tractor like a surgeon's assistant.

"Hand me that wrench, will you?" Mike says to Jimmy, "and a couple of them sockets."

In a moment, Mike turns from the stomach of the tractor like a surgeon removing an organ. He sets the carburetor on the workbench. The thick metal is shaped like a fat elbow and caked in grease. The carburetor's no bigger than an old boot, but the part is essential to the whole.

"Screwdriver?" Mike motions to Jimmy, "No. The flathead."

"How is everybody Jimmy?" asks Uncle Charlie.

"Ah, we're doing just fine," says Jimmy.

"That ain't what he told me," protests Mike, lifting his eyes from the carburetor.

"Well, all be!" says Uncle Charlie with a toothy grin, "Do tell, Jimmy."

Jimmy blushes and squirms, not expecting to air his frustrations during shop talk.

"Well, uh . . . since we had the baby, things have just been . . . off, you know?"

"What'd you expect, Jimmy?" says Uncle Charlie, "it's a big change going from two to three and that fast. Boy, son." Uncle Charlie shakes his head and says, "You got your work cut out for you."

"Yeah, I know—goes with the territory."

"So, what's the problem?" asks Uncle Charlie.

"Since Olivia's been back at work, I come home, and it's nothing but dishes and diapers and laundry, and the next day it's all the same. And the next—just like it."

"So, what's the problem?" repeats Uncle Charlie, smiling.

"Something's just . . . off. I don't know," Jimmy sighs.

"Hold your breath, Charlie. Already told him about the gratitude list," says Mike as his fingers check the gaskets.

"Oh, I bet you did."

"He still needs five more, though," replies Mike.

"So let me guess," says Uncle Charlie, "wife, kids, job, house, health, all that, right?"

"Just about," answers Jimmy.

"So, what's the problem? Why do you even need five more?" asks Uncle Charlie.

Mike smiles from the workbench. Jimmy shifts his weight against the tractor tires.

"I just get, uh, irritated, you know? Short fuse, fed up with the littlest things."

"Whooo, now we gettin' somewhere!" says Mike, who looks up from the dissected carburetor with a smile, "please, do continue."

"Feel like I'm out of touch or out of patience," confesses Jimmy.

"And let me guess," says Uncle Charlie, "at work, you're at your best, but Olivia and kids get the brunt of it?"

Jimmy nods.

"Hmm?" questions Mike, staring at Jimmy.

"Yes," Jimmy says, "yes, sir."

"Couldn't hear that head nod," says Mike.

It's a line Mike picked up from his late father. He uses it weekly in the A.A. meetings to help members own their issues.

"Sounds like your family's getting your leftovers, Jimmy," says Uncle Charlie.

"You're not wrong. Kind of goes with the territory," replies Jimmy.

"So, what're you gonna do about it?" asks Uncle Charlie.

"Not sure yet."

Mike reassembles the pieced-apart carburetor. The ratchet zips and ticks as he remounts the unit. The part seems small and insignificant to the whole. Still, Mike knows for the tractor to properly function, every piece matters.

"Better figure out what's missing and fix it, Jimmy. All them parts need to work together," says Mike.

"Go ahead and jump up there," Mike motions to Uncle Charlie, "let's give it a go."

Uncle Charlie turns to Jimmy, "Go on up, son."

Jimmy jumps at the opportunity to escape the spotlight and climbs into the pan seat.

"All right, Jimmy, give it a go. It's in neutral, right? Make sure that fuel valve's on."

"Okay, got it," says Jimmy.

"Flip that ignition switch, set the throttle about a third of the way," says Mike.

"Okay, um, yeah, there we go. I think I got it."

"Okay, now, pull the choke rod."

"Okay!"

"Now pull that starter rod!"

The engine stalls.

"You see, Jimmy, it all needs to work together just right. Little here, little there, and the whole thing comes together—or it doesn't."

Mike moves around the machine, twisting and turning various valves and knobs. After he adjusts the air/fuel mixture, Mike says,

"Okay, let's try that again."

Jimmy repeats the sequence, and the tractor barks and coughs but keeps chugging.

"Give it a second and let go of that choke rod!" yells Mike over the noise.

Jimmy nods.

A moment later, Jimmy releases the choke rod. The engine growls and runs smooth and proper. Uncle Charlie yells out in triumph,

"There it is!"

"She's purrin' like a kitten!" Mike yells back.

Jimmy looks down from behind the wheel and beams.

"Goes with the territory!" yells Jimmy.

"The hell it does, Jimmy!" shouts Mike, "We rebuilt the territory!"

The ride back is quiet. Not silent, but quiet. Uncle Charlie had thanked them for the time, the help, and the conversation. Before leaving the barn, they shook hands with their sandpaper palms and jawed at Jimmy more. But Uncle Charlie left it with,

"Give my love to Olivia and the kids. And don't be no stranger now, Jimmy, you hear?"

Jimmy knew it was Uncle Charlie's way of offering everything of himself to help in any way. He is a good man, salt of the earth.

Few words are uttered between the hardware store owner and Jimmy, who sits beside him in the truck, putting the pieces of his life together. The diesel engine hums over the silence. The wipers clear the snow from view.

Jimmy wonders about the tractor. For all he feels and knows, the tractor seems secondary now. As if . . . was it even there? Of course, it was. But Jimmy himself feels more taken apart and put back together in the process. It's not like something was missing the whole time—it was always there—just needing to be tuned. How can he ever explain this to Olivia?

I went with Mike to fix Uncle Charlie's tractor and came back more . . . what?

Whole? Focused? Better?

He feels different, sure. But how to describe it? It's too big a word for anything. But it's how everything ought to be. Lighter, un-burdened. More than his mind has changed. Something in the depth of his everything has shifted—like the fine-tuning of a carburetor.

He sees more than ever the problem—Olivia and the kids deserve more than his leftovers. They've gotten the meager good bits of him and the full brunt of his flaws. They deserve more. Or better. That's the truth.

Jimmy thinks of Mike, twisting and turning all the valves and knobs—and he thinks of all the things in him that need a fix. Who wants a husband who's always selfish? He's always coming through the door irritated, something upsetting him. Who wants a dad who just barks orders and doles out punishment? He's tired of the threats and empty promises. He's sick of his ever-shifting moods. No, he realizes, they deserve so much more. His time, energy, focus—his love.

Jimmy pictures them in his mind—like from the photo they framed of the day at the lake. Olivia's dark hair caught in the wind. The boys with the gaps in their teeth. And plump little Ginny, she must've been what, a few months old? It was just last summer, but now he can't help but see all that's broken down in him—the irritation, the finger-pointing, the blame-placing, and letting frustration get the best of him. They deserve more. Because they are truly the best thing about him.

It's thanks, he feels. The gratitude list could go on and on—Oliva and the kids—a job, a house, friends, health, food, clothes—it's a new thanks he feels for everything. But so, too, it's completeness, wholeness—a peace—he guesses. It doesn't quite go with the territory. Or maybe it does—to change everything about the territory.

They pass rows of houses and gnarled, naked trees. Across the white wasteland, a red barn juts up from the snow. A billboard streams past the passenger window selling everything anyone could ever want and nothing they ever need. It goes with the territory—it wears you down and lulls you to sleep. You follow the same old tracks in the snow until you wake up decades from now, waking up for the last time and realizing how long you've been asleep. But Jimmy thinks about the tractor and Mike's words—

We've rebuilt the territory.

Well, something has. Or someone.

This was never quite about the tractor, was it?

Five minutes from now, he'll step out into the snow. He'll thank Mike and slam the screeching truck door. He'll turn to face his home and those in there who love him—and then what?

Notes to Chapter 1

Chapter 1 opens the series of short stories by focusing on the biblical experience of *hesed* portrayed in story form. This story seeks to capture the meaning of *hesed* as "steadfast love," as it is often translated. It also highlights several other nuances and experiences of *hesed*: strength, commitment, love, mercy, fortitude, generosity, and kindness. The attempt here is to describe the essence of *hesed* in story form—in an emotive manner of understanding the biblical use of the term to create a fuller scope for imagination and praxis. The prophet Hosea employs *hesed* to describe God as a father teaching his child to walk and carrying him in his arms.[1] Jeremiah does likewise as he pictures a father whose undying love moves to hold his lost son again with fervent emotion.[2] This parental expression of *hesed* in both prophetic works is what this short story seeks to display.

The formula for this story is linear narration with a series of flashbacks. The flashbacks emphasize the unending steadfast love and commitment of *hesed* despite the drastic change in circumstance (from the innocence of boyhood to guilt on death row).

Chapter 1's story arc is of a single mother who every Saturday boards a bus to take a three-hour trip to visit her son on death row. Flashbacks occur as she continues with her constant Saturday visiting routine. The flashbacks do not provide a sense of enabling love or naïve ignorance (e.g., my son is innocent). Instead, the flashbacks show her grappling with the stark change in circumstance and life's

1. Eichrodt, *Theology of the Old Testament*, 238.

2. Jer 31:3.

altered trajectory while simultaneously continuing in steadfast love. As the mother embodies *hesed*, her actions are altogether loyally committed in love for her son regardless of anything.

The story describes the struggle of a single mother who sets out to visit her son on a cold Saturday morning. She arises early to endure the frigid conditions and board a bus that will take her across state lines to a maximum-security prison. Her journey is tiresome, challenging, and of utmost purpose for her. The journey she habitually embarks on highlights *hesed* as an action or an event rather than an attitude.[3] Along with the "strength" and "fortitude" that describe her hesed, kindness characterizes the mother's behavior toward every character (especially in her interactions with the bus driver and the deputy). She operates as *hesed* with a keen sense of familiarity and kinship that goes far deeper than a typical passenger/bus driver or visitor/corrections officer relations might. Each aspect of the journey—her familiar seat on the bus, to memorizing the signage in the waiting room, to knowing the exact number of steps and "every scuff in the flooring, every scratch along the wall" in the maze-like prison—displays an acute awareness and habitual rhythm characteristic of constant steadfast love. The deputy also has the mother's credentials memorized, emphasizing her consistent routine to outsiders' perspectives.

The first flashback the mother experiences in the waiting room brings her back to a lunch date when her son was a child at a hole-in-the-wall restaurant called Lucky's. The purpose of the flashback is to show a happier time, long before death row, when she also consistently displayed generosity and love. Nothing in her behavior causes her son's change in behavior and action (i.e., ending up on death row)—she is *hesed* with constant steadfast love.

Each flashback ends with a cold and sometimes harsh interruption as the mother returns to her unfortunate reality. However, the mother has learned that although the circumstance is not ideal, this grim environment where her son dwells has become a place "she'd rather be than anywhere." A flashback of her son working construction and another reflecting on his actions in an elevator

3. Ziegert, "What Is חֶ֫סֶד?," 711.

sets up a heartache for what could have been in his life. The memory also reveals metaphorically how there are buttons in life that cannot be unpressed. Despite this painful and complex reality, the mother's *hesed* remains unmoved and undiminished.

After the exhaustive journey to and through the prison, the mother waits for a thirty-minute visitation with her son. *Hesed* is also present in her waiting, such as with pregnancy, and in the devotion and expectation that awaits. When the mother has a short interaction with her son over the phone, separated by thick glass, there is no pretending that he is innocent of any crime. There is the gut-wrenching reality that he is guilty of his actions. Nonetheless, she displays loyalty and a "loving constancy of a covenant far surpassing human standards."[4]

The interaction between mother and son is brief. It centers around a conversation regarding Ernest Hemingway's *The Old Man and the Sea*. Hemingway's work thematically represents the mother's unyielding commitment. The mother is just like Santiago, the fisherman who refuses to give up despite troubling circumstances, even after the catch of his life is devoured by sharks. The visit quickly passes, and in a moment, she retraces the same familiar steps out of the facility, teary-eyed but not neglecting the *hesed* of her lovingkindness.

Even as the mother exits the prison and makes her way back to the bus, she stops at Swenson's Diner, leaving a generous tip in the spirit of her *hesed*. Then the story closes after her three-hour trip home on the bus when she steps into the cold and resolves to do the same next week. The hope, confidence, and resolve of *hesed* define her entire character.[5] Regardless of external circumstances and in full awareness of the grim situation (her son on death row) the mother's loyalty is such that her life orders around her absolute commitment to love.

4. Eichrodt, *Theology of the Old Testament*, 238.

5. Gen 19:19; 39:21.

Notes to Chapter 2

THE FOCUS OF THIS chapter is the biblical notion of *hamartia*—often translated as "sin." *Hamartia* is the most frequent word in the New Testament for "sin" and the Septuagint (526 times).[1] The term images an archer missing a target they should have hit and consequently hitting an outside region they should not have. However, this chapter aims to capture the nuances and experiences of *hamartia* as "a mistake," "an error," and "the things we get wrong." Beyond the "missing the mark" nuance, *hamartia* describes dynamic power with a cosmic scope that enslaves humanity and brings about spiritual and physical death. Chapter 2 seeks to display this expression in the weakness of human flesh and in the failure of humans to recognize the God to whom all creation points.

This short story follows a "slice of life" formula that focuses on seemingly random moments, scenes, and observations. The interrupting radio and television broadcasts incrementally demoralize the mood. Equally, the main character's attitude sinks in morale, optimism, and will to live—as might be experienced with the nature of sin. In short, *hamartia* is an evil, destructive power dragging everyone and everything low.

Chapter 2's arc is of a lonely, hopeless alcoholic contemplating the end of his own life. After losing his job, he aimlessly drives around town, avoiding sobriety. As he drives, his thoughts on numbing the lonely hopelessness are interrupted by dreadful radio broadcasts. The broadcasts depict the depressed state of the world—clearly touched by sin's presence and devastation. The main

1. Silker, *Sin in the New Testament*, 18.

character's life deepens in apathy and skepticism, and it sinks to an all-time low before the story's close, which somehow leaves him in a church parking lot.

The story begins with a description of the main character, Paul, drunk-driving in his miserable, smoke-stained pickup truck littered with beer cans. His drinking paints an image of sin as all-consuming and addicting. While drinking in moderation is in no way sinful, Paul's approach embodies how alcohol can become a life-ruining object.[2] The trash and filth of his truck cab reflect an image of nearing destruction or degradation at the very least. Paul's environment reflects a desperate and foreboding situation. He suddenly swerves and nearly jeopardizes his ability to keep the rusted truck on the road when he makes passing eye contact with the mother from the previous chapter.

A talk radio broadcast interrupts Paul's drunken state to describe a gruesome scene. A mother's neglect (contrasting *hesed*) kills her ten-year-old boy. This aspect of *hamartia* within the broadcast shows how wrong actions and tragic negligence lead to harrowing consequences that cause destruction and, ultimately, death. However, even in the grisly detailing of the murder, the broadcaster's tone abruptly shifts—"And now onto sports!" This tone shift highlights the widespread resolve to brush past (versus dealing with) the nature of sin. This avoidance of confronting sin is itself sin. Silence and avoidance of sin is, in fact, a sin by allowance or immobility.

Paul continues drinking and driving and is again interrupted by a radio broadcast. The radio segment details a military airstrike causing collateral damage in Afghanistan, claiming the lives of three women and eleven children. *Hamartia,* in this broadcast, depicts the detached-from-reality political commentary and spin that seeks to assuage geopolitical destruction and bloodshed. This nuance of *hamartia* displays sin as a collective defect in character, a punishable vice, a moral failing that brings disastrous results.[3] The reality here that everyone is "under the power of sin" (Rom 3:9) is something that the drunk-driving Paul attempts to dull. He

2. Eph 5:17.

3. Owiredu, "Sin Is a Person," 90.

goes to the liquor store to refuel his downward spiral with more beer and cigarettes.

On his precarious way to the liquor store, a third radio broadcast fills his cab—a perpetrator committing extensive identity fraud is arrested by the F.B.I. While the F.B.I. is taking in another criminal, another nuance of *hamartia* reveals how sin is an active agent that dwells within and motivates by taking one's will captive.[4]

As Paul arrives at the liquor store, alluring advertising meets him. The glowing beer signs feed his addiction, and the images of scantily clad cheerleaders promise everything but only deliver empty hopes and base desires. The deception and enticement of marketing show *hamartia* personified as an active agent, a cosmic power or force working in the world for the ill that "enslaves" (Rom 6:6, 16–17; 7:25) and exercises "dominion in your mortal bodies" (Rom 6:12).

Paul and the disinterested store clerk watch a breaking story unfold on a mute television screen inside the liquor store. In this domestic issue, an ex-husband has barricaded himself with his ex-wife and kids in a mobile home. As SWAT engages and unleashes a German shepherd into the residence, shots ring out, and the situation instantly turns grim. The video feed cuts back to the studio, where the news anchors are shocked by the outcome. Their shock results from witnessing brutality and experiencing *hamartia* as lawlessness (1 John 3:4)—breaking the divine law through action or inaction, speech, and thought. The customary question, "How could someone do such a thing?" is answered by *hamartia* as lawlessness.

Paul continues to induce his inebriation upon leaving the store, staving off sobriety. Such methods epitomize how sin operates to dull, distract, or blind the senses (spiritually, mentally, physically). The continuation of his drunk driving also embodies *hamartia* as violating society's moral and ethical ideals.[5] This carelessness and disregard are a sin endangering himself and anyone else nearby.

4. Rom 7:17, 20.

5. Owiredu, "Sin Is a Person," 90.

Paul entertains the possibility of death, and the recent job loss serves as an image relating the wages of sin to death.[6] Without the wages from his work, his life has reached an empty state. His job, in a sense, was the only thing keeping him motivated. The trajectory of his life is unrestrained disillusionment. The wages of such a lifestyle yield death. He considers stopping at Gino's bar and escalating to hard liquor. But it has a way of depressing him further, darkening his thoughts toward suicide. The theme of suicide in this chapter highlights the effects of *hamartia*, representing the potential rock bottom of Paul's interaction with sin and suffering the effects of it. Thoughts of suicide, as depicted in this chapter, are the result of despair (the act of giving up hope) and the all-out consumption of sin.

Sin manifests in almost personal terms as a ruling power (Rom 5:12) when Paul dismays, having failed to grab a few pornographic magazines. This dabbling in sin gives Paul a momentary escape from loneliness until it rages back vigorously. The capacity for the power of sin to entice through desire and bring about transgression and death is characteristic of the inner battle Paul (unknowingly) is experiencing between the power of sin and the power of God's Spirit.[7] Whether he knows it or not, Paul is driving through a world scarred by sin and, simultaneously, being redeemed by God.

But even as a final radio broadcast relays the news of sex trafficking, further demonstrating sin and the human condition, God appears absent from the entire scene. Everything is subject to sin (Gal 3:22); people serve it (Rom 6:6) and are sold into its service (Rom 7:14). In this chapter, sin arises in specific actions, as a general state, and as a concrete force or power. All the while, it seems God is absent, that is, until Paul winds up in a church parking lot with a truck that's dead. Paul's experience with and involvement in sin—the distraction, active rebellion, and the life of sin entangling him are ripe for a transformation.

6. Rom 6:23.

7. Silker, *Sin in the New Testament*, 114.

Notes to Chapter 3

Chapter 3 uses a story to express the biblical experience of *pis-tis*—often translated as "faith." This short story follows a formula of a "slice of life" in which the story's character, theme, and setting develop with a minimal story arc. This formula expresses *pistis* as faith within the ordinary. This faith is transforming, life-giving, and essential. As displayed in this story, *pistis* in action is the elemental substance to the rhythms of life that strengthens and confirms belief and reason.

While minimal and unresolved, the story's arc is of a mother who performs household and professional tasks with excellence and dedication. A friend is about to visit, so preparations are being made for his arrival. However, the larger picture is of a faithful life of marriage, motherhood, leadership, teamwork, family, and decision-making. Each aspect of the story correlates to *pistis* on a practical level.

Pistis in the biblical narrative is a sense of "pledge" or "evidence" on which subjective confidence or belief may appropriately be based.[1] In short, *pistis* is trustful belief.[2] The source, person, and application of *pistis* vary throughout the New Testament (e.g., the *pistis Christou* debate arguing for the "faith in Christ" or the "faithfulness of Christ" in Rom 3:21–26; Gal. 2:16, 20, 3:22; Eph. 3:12; Phil.3:9). "Belief" and "faith," albeit different from one another, can provide an overarching theme of the New Testament term *pistis*. However, *pistis* further carries the meaning of "conviction,"

1. Hay, "Pistis," 461.

2. Heb 11:1, 6; 2 Cor 5:7; 1 Cor 13:13; Rom 3:22, Eph 4:13; Matt 8:10; Gal 5:22.

"steadfastness," and "loyalty."[3] Chapter 3 emphasizes the trustful belief, loyalty, and commitment communicated by the New Testament's usage of *pistis.*

In this story, "faith" (*pistis*) is the trustful belief that Margot repeats in her daily activity. This act of *pistis* in seemingly menial tasks amounts to a life defined by faithfulness. A *pistis* expression of trust and confidence to behave in a particular way is present in Margot's character as she moves through each scene.

The story opens with Margot preparing a room for their friend from high school, Roy, who is visiting for their high school reunion. It is with intentional care that she readies the room. All her efforts may go unseen, but they certainly are well-spent. This effort on Margot's part correlates to the life of *pistis* as being the way of integrity and righteousness, even when no one is watching. With everything set out for Roy's arrival, Margot faithfully moves on to care for her newborn baby. The baby formula thematically represents how *pistis* is the means to survival, the substance of what is hoped for, and the evidence of things not seen (i.e., the hope for growth and maturation). Providing and sustaining a new life parallels cultivating *pistis* in one's life.

After setting the baby down, Margot begins baking a cornbread casserole. She is familiar with the process and measurements. Furthermore, Margot is confident that the ingredients will spread and cause the casserole to come together. The baking powder produces expansion and works through the casserole like a mustard seed in good soil, producing thirty, sixty, or even a hundred times more goodness. This image relates to the back-to-back parables of Jesus in Luke 13:18–21 (the mustard seed and the woman with yeast and dough). *Pistis,* in this manner, expresses the outworking and expansion of faith and is followed up by the roles in which Margot and her husband Sam operate efficiently and faithfully.

The household chores (which Margot and Sam do interchangeably without subscribing to gender roles) are viewed considering a quote from her mother, who once told Margot that "Repetition strengthens and confirms." *Pistis,* therefore, is that which, when

3. Fredriksen, "Paul's Letter to the Romans," 801.

repeated, strengthens and confirms behavior, patterns, or entire life trajectories. A task as simple as folding, sorting, moving, and storing laundered clothing is an opportunity for faithfulness and reflection.

Further insight into Margot's professional background reveals that she has a persevering attitude driven by strong convictions. Her coworkers feel the pinch of her absence because she is a defining presence within the work community as she shatters glass ceilings and functions as a force for good. As with faith which is a gift received (Eph. 2:8–9), Margot's attitude/persona/faithful endurance is received from and instilled in her by her mother. Margot's mother worked multiple jobs and rose through the ranks with a dogged determination to survive and provide. So too it is with *pistis*—the endeavor of a faithful life requires a dogged determination to withstand, overcome, and walk through life's toughest challenges.

The scene at the mailbox represents how to make decisions faithfully and function in a world of distraction. What is essential in one's life manages to inform decision-making. The countless distractions fed into one's life daily (i.e., symbolized by a mailbox and everything within it) can drown out the essentiality of *pistis*.

The closing scene of the story reflects on a flashback Margot has. While ending a conversation with Sam, she hears in the background the whining brakes of an oncoming vehicle at the airport. The sound transports her to a traumatic memory of a near-death accident. With her pelvis shattered and an uphill climb to recovery, Margot's experience symbolizes the reality that *pistis* is rarely easy, full of hardship, and all the while worth every obstacle. For *pistis* is precisely her experience eight years after the accident and two babies since. *Pistis* moves mountains, and this repetition strengthens and confirms. This *pistis* is a force not merely perpetuated by the human condition to be resilient. It is the reality of Matt 17:20—"If you have faith (in God) the size of a mustard seed, you will say to this mountain, 'Move from here to there,' and it will move; and nothing will be impossible for you."

Notes to Chapter 4

Chapter 4 explores a story that focuses on the biblical experience of *qadosh* ("holy," "sacred," and "set apart" are the typical renderings). In this story, *qadosh* is an otherworldly experience of being intentionally set apart and ultimately refers to a quality that God alone fully possesses. The plot of chapter 4 seeks to engage the imagination with *qadosh* by expressing that which is special and set apart for a specific purpose. The story's action puts the main character in confrontation with a church environment defined by *qadosh*.

The formula for this short story involves a vignette of Paul Barnes (from chapter 2) having a sobering experience with "the holy" at a funeral service he happens to stumble into. The story's arc involves Paul abruptly sobering from a drunken state as he enters a church where a funeral service is ongoing. Paul begins to interact with an event characterized by holiness. The spiritual traditions and practices (song, Scripture, prayer, response, art, community, imagery) contain an otherworldly, unique quality set apart. The entire experience leaves him with a decision that impacts his past, present, and future.

Chapter 4 begins where chapter 2 left off—with Paul in a drunken state in a church parking lot. This chapter reveals his full name as "Paul Barnes," loosely based on Hemingway's Jake Barnes from *The Sun Also Rises*. Jake Barnes is a young American expatriate working in a Paris newspaper office in Hemingway's work. As an injured veteran of WWI, he lives irresponsibly and drinks heavily with friends whom he seems careless about. Overall, Jake (and here in this story, Paul) represents the worst of the Lost

Generation—irresponsible, bitter, and aimless. His life appears over before it has begun.

However, everything begins to transform in this "Damascus road" experience for Paul. Instead of being blinded, he receives new sight into the *qadosh*. After being nearly floored and struck stone-cold sober upon entering the church, Paul contemplates and tries to make sense of the striking new images. The choir members look like ghosts. The incense is magical, and the organ and songs have an overpowering influence. This effect of experiencing the holy is that the environment has changed precisely because God—the *qadosh* indescribable, omnipotent, invisible, everlasting deity—has chosen it to be so. The revelation of God communicates to Paul through the holiness of ritual and tradition. It is reminiscent of the Tabernacle and Temple, where the vessels in the sanctuary become *qadosh* because they have been rendered "sanctified."[1]

While the scene displays purity and otherworldliness, Paul reminds himself of those "ordinary folks from the community" involved in it—engaged in being "set apart." He ponders if the ordinary, mundane things suddenly transform into something otherworldly or if the otherworldly was always there in the mundane and ordinary, and he never saw it before. This line of thought relates to the quality of *qadosh*. It is reminiscent of purification at the center of the priestly role in ancient Israel. Such acts of purification involve the priest intentionally moving items (people, places, time, objects) from common to holy and distinguishing between each categorically.[2] Therefore, when Paul hears a choir of "ordinary folks from the community," he is experiencing the touch and transformation of the holy. The "priestly" activities of *qadosh* in the scene (choir members, the priest, the organist, the usher) influence his life and the somber atmosphere. For instance, the words spoken by the priest are Scripture (thus set apart as *qadosh*), and the reading and responding contribute to faith-building and reassurance.

Leviticus 10:10–11 describes the priest's task of distinguishing between the holy and common and the unclean and clean. The role

1. Exod 28:36.
2. Ezek 44:23.

is also to help people discover what is holy and not—ultimately, to help them understand how to behave considering that information. However, the ongoing holy realization produces an encounter with his mortality and familiarity with death for Paul. As he stands at the threshold, merely spectating the ongoing funeral for a young boy who took his own life (his boss's son, it turns out), an usher welcomes him to take a seat. This action thematically "ushers" him into deeper engagement and interaction with the holy. As he sits beside a stained-glass window that depicts Jesus calling Lazarus from the tomb, the glass imagery parallels Paul's experience of being called from his own tomb.

Paul interacts with the holy as the service continues. *Qadosh* creates a space for him to reflect, dwell in memory, and experience exhilaration. Paul witnesses how simplicity can also characterize as holy (as with Xavier Simmons, the basketball coach, and his "words [that] aren't poetic or religious, but they're heartfelt and set apart"). Xavier speaks in a "set apart" way because it separates the "fluff" from reality. There is an assisting clarity and truth ("a strategy and vision in the simplest of terms [and] a purity present") in his words that can parallel how the holiness of God cuts through facades and pretenses.

At the close, Paul reflects on the mystery unfolding before him—the otherworldly transformation. The boy's picture beside the casket becomes like a mirror reflecting Paul's life should he continue down his desolate trajectory. However, the situation grows complex with new possibilities after being introduced to an experience of *qadosh*. Since God himself is set apart, *qadosh*, those who follow his ways are also *qadosh*.[3] This notion and mystery of the holy leave Paul with a decision to continue in the way he was going or to engage deeper in *qadosh*. This decision is an action that an encounter with the holy produces because, as Jerome states, "Holiness consists in total self-offering."[4]

3. Bloom, "Legacy of 'Sacred' and 'Profane,'" 119.

4. Leinhard, *Exodus*, 176.

Notes to Chapter 5

Chapter 5 presents a story that embodies the biblical experience of *chara* ("joy"). *Chara* is an experience of joy distinct from happiness in that happiness is a feeling based on circumstances, whereas joy (*chara*) is an attitude that defines circumstances. This short story aims to mirror this notion to communicate that although the situation may not be ideal, the God within every event works for good, which is joy-inducing.

The story arc of chapter 5 involves a son (high school basketball coach Xavier Simmons) visiting his sickly mother after the funeral for one of his players. Both mother and son recount hardships ongoing in their lives. In doing so, *chara* works to shape and define their circumstances.

The formula for this short story is an ongoing linear narration paired with extensive dialogue. Chapter 5 picks up where the previous chapter left off but focuses on a new character introduced in chapter 4's funeral service.

Visiting her tiny, one-bedroom apartment, Xavier sees his mother struggling through various circumstances, frail and cancerous. She is Marsha from Lucky's, the burger restaurant in chapter 1, but years down the road and now toting an oxygen canister with her wherever she goes in the apartment. Throughout the chapter, oxygen represents joy in doing hard things (i.e., breathing through difficult circumstances).

As Xavier enters the room, it is clear his mother is a sickly "shut-in," unable to escape from the confines of her apartment. Regardless, this inhibiting circumstance does not stop her from exploring the world through a monthly subscription to National Geographic. She expresses the attitude, "How am I supposed to know about Egypt if I can't go there?" with Frank McCourt's line: "You might be poor, your shoes might be broken, but your mind is a palace."

For Marsha, *chara* comes with a world of possibilities even when the regular options are impossible. Despite her limiting circumstances, her excitement for exploration (black holes, jaguars, deep-sea octopuses) continues. The magazine article featuring the deep-sea octopus (whose eggs take over five years to hatch) reflects the joy (*chara*) of motherhood present in Marsha's life. The search in National Geographic also represents the kingdom of heaven, like a merchant searching for fine pearls or a treasure finder in a field.[1] When found, the joyful transformation is the experience of being caught up by something rare, fine, and beautiful, holding the person in its grasp.[2] Throughout the interaction between mother and son, Marsha has the resolve of surprising joy. She somehow has a treasure that solves all her problems (e.g., the treasure finder) and the intensely emotional experience of a merchant who finds the object of their search.[3]

Over coffee, Marsha and Xavier recount the events of the funeral for Xavier's basketball player, who died of suicide (Mark, the boss's son that Paul Barnes referenced in chapter 2 and 4). Xavier carries the heaviness of the loss, and the tragedy of life extinguished so soon and in such heartbreaking circumstances. However, in the heart of tragedy, the simple sharing of a meal, a bit of laughter, and embracing have a way of producing the attitude-defining circumstance of *chara*.

Marsha's living situation is not ideal, with neighborhood crime and violence rising. Her troubling circumstances (health failure, crime, violence, isolation, financial pressure) should suffocate. But she discovered how joy (*chara*) is the oxygen for doing hard things. As Xavier processes the difficulty of his situation throughout the

1. Matt 13:44–46.
2. Waters, "Getting More," 431.
3. Waters, "Getting More," 430.

story, he is exposed to his mother's joyous resolve despite her troubles. In this interaction, Marsha becomes, in a way, oxygen also for him. The oxygen is joy—a sign of a future reality more than it is a good of this present time—for this act parallels "Enter[ing] into the joy of the Lord" (Matt 25:23), which is not consoling and casual so much as it is cosmic and eschatological.[4] The joy keeps Marsha going, just as oxygen physically keeps her alive.

An entire episode of joy-building or joy-inducing behavior marks the conversation between mother and son. Marsha is like Elizabeth (Luke 1) and Mary (Luke 2), who experience an inaugurated joy with the purpose of sharing. Marsha likewise pours joy into the life of her son. Xavier returns to her home after the funeral like the prodigal of Luke 15, not bankrupt by his wild pursuits but emotionally impoverished by the heaviness of ongoing tragedy. His mother (like the father of Luke 15) greets him joyfully and prepares a feast for him. Although Marsha is a cancerous, disabled shut-in, she displays for her son the "paradoxical element" in the Christian's joy that it runs highest in the face of testing and imminent dissolution.[5] She embodies this "paradoxical element" by rejoicing in weakness (2 Cor 13:9) and counting it all joy when meeting trials (Jas 1:2).[6]

4. Sloyan, "Joy of Christ," 92.

5. Sloyan, "Joy of Christ," 96.

6. Sloyan, "Joy of Christ," 96.

Notes to Chapter 6

The biblical experience of *tov* is the focus of chapter 6. *Tov* is typically translated as "good," "goodness," or "beauty." The storyline of chapter 6 seeks to convey the essence of *tov* as that which produces life and contains the potential for more life within it. *Tov* expresses whatever enhances, promotes, produces, or is conducive to life.

The formula for this short story is mainly dialogue paired with an ongoing linear narration that ends with an abrupt cliffhanger. This story continues chapter 3's interaction with Margot and *pistis*. Chapter 6's story arc involves two old friends conversing and reflecting on the past, present, and future. As their conversation unfolds, it is unmissable how opposite the two have become. The driver, Sam (Margot's husband), presents a *tov* perspective of good, goodness, and beauty—while the passenger, Roy, finds fault in everything. The story aims to show the distinction between "good" and factors that define "goodness" upon a backdrop void of good.

The chapter opens with Roy, a successful business executive delivering disparaging remarks about his friend Sam's minivan. As a character representing *tov*, Sam has driven to the Los Angeles airport to pick up his old friend Roy who is in town for their twentieth high school reunion. The minivan and everything that define Sam portrays his character as self-sacrificing, parental, and generous. With Roy, it is the opposite. Sam laughs off Roy's cutting remarks and gives a *tov*-like concern and attention to his friend's travel experience. Never in the story does Roy reciprocate any regard or attention to the details or happenings of Sam's life. In response to Sam's interest, Roy spouts pure negativity and disdain for marginal inconveniences that prove frustrating to his privileged life (a weak cocktail, having to encounter individuals outside of first-class, curious children, being bumped by luggage, and having his warm nuts spilled). Roy's privileged, high society sensitivities are irked by the ordinary and common—thus revealing ignorance of *tov*. In his tirade about the supposed incompetence of the flight attendant, Roy's last name, Macomber, is revealed. This surname relates to Hemingway's short story, "The Short Happy Life of Francis Macomber." In Hemingway's work, Francis Macomber is a cowardly but wealthy sport-hunter who, when he encounters a lion on a hunt, does not shoot and instead runs. Francis Macomber is a failed character. Even the next day, when he demonstrates his bravery, he is killed at the moment of his triumph. In chapter 6, Roy represents a figure who seems sure of himself and confident of what *tov* or "good" might be. Still, internally he is cowardly and inept when it comes to *tov*.

Sam continues with his questions as the friends travel northward along the southern California coast. Roy speaks at length about his success in business and accumulation of wealth. When Sam, a high school history teacher, tries to talk about his life, Roy rudely dismisses it and continues his self-centered monologue. Regardless, Sam continues his interest in Roy's life, even though he has no clue or interest about business profit margins and shareholders' equity. This interest is precisely because of *tov*.

Sam's goodness and generosity toward Roy in providing him with a free place to stay and home-cooked meals are met with a cold indifference and more "higher class" plans (the Four Seasons instead of a futon and a business meeting with a potential client instead of cornbread casserole with an old friend and his family). Roy is also indifferent to Sam's condolences for the loss of his father—he interrupts Sam to take a phone call. The call shows Roy barking on the phone at an employee he treats with hostility and carelessness. Oppositely, Sam's character develops as an individual careless about such "striving after the wind." He desires to help people—to be an influence, a positive role model for the kids, seeing his life like a seed that produces an orchard.

As their conversation continues, Roy flaunts his wealth, toying with buying another vacation home. This is compared to Sam's struggle to afford rent. Roy also voices negligence regarding relationships, whereas Sam is a committed husband and self-sacrificing father. Roy's relational probing about how Sam must be unsatisfied is the only time Roy concerns himself with Sam's life. However, the opposite of *tov* displayed in Roy's questioning reveals a bleak and apathetic perspective. Even as the two reflect on old friends from high school, as Sam shows tenderness for relationships, Roy shows a shallow rashness.

When the minivan passes along a stretch of the Pacific Coast Highway where the service drops, Roy cannot physically or emotionally connect with the landscape's *tov* ("beauty"). Instead, he "struggles relentlessly to manufacture a cell tower's notice of his importance." Then on a section of road outside of cell service, Sam stops to help a teenager with a flat tire. This inconvenience frustrates Roy even more than the flight attendant's weak cocktails. In his goodness, Sam tries to help the stranded driver and assist by teaching the teenager how to repair the problem himself. The wait boils Roy's blood by the minute until he can contain it no longer. He does not even bother checking for oncoming traffic in his self-centeredness, which ultimately leads to his sudden end.

The abrupt ending provides a warning reflective of Proverbs 2:20–22: "Therefore walk in the way of the good (*tov*), and keep to the paths of the just. For the upright will abide in the land, and the innocent will remain in it; but the wicked will be cut off from the land, and the treacherous will be rooted out of it." Furthermore, the entire story draws two contradicted pictures: one of goodness that reflects the generosity and beauty of Genesis 1–2, and the other of Ecclesiastes with meaningless humanistic efforts to control.

Notes to Chapter 7

Chapter 7 focuses on expressing the biblical experience of *elpis*—often translated as "hope"—using a story. This short story follows a formula of a linear story told in the past tense leading up to a present moment. Along with defining *elpis* as "hope," the nuance of *elpis* as "confident expectation" is also present within the story. The story's theme communicates how circumstances may disappoint, but hope does not. Hope placed in the proper place/entity is life-giving.

The story's arc is of a young couple who, at seven months pregnant, face the shocking reality that they must undergo an emergency c-section. A trying time in the Neonatal Intensive Care Unit that follows tests their resolve, faith, and relationship. In every "hurdle," they are surrounded by uncertainty and fear. However, with hope, they experience confident expectations grounded in truth, experience, and grit.

Elpis in the biblical narrative is not a pie-in-the-sky fantasy or wishful thinking but a concrete, confident expectation of what God has done, does and will do.[1] This story seeks to do likewise in its representation of hope. In this story, "hope" (*elpis*) is the confident expectation not of fairytale dreams but of concrete realities (i.e., what you can always expect to be true and worthy of expectation). This nuance of hope plays an upfront role in the story as it comes up against doubt, uncertainty, shock, fear, and even impossibility. A biblical hope of confident expectation that does not disappoint is

1. Rom 5:5; 1 Cor 9:10; 2 Cor 3:12; Eph 1:18; Phil 1:20; Col 1:23, 27; 1 Thess 5: 8; Heb 3:6; 1 Pet 3:15; 1 John 3:3.

present within the young couple's attitude, even when they waiver in the stress of long days and weeks at the NICU. Their basis for operating in this way is to understand that God and the things of God are a concrete reality, not a pie-in-the-sky fantasy.

The story opens with a shocking message carrying countless emotions—*"Get here fast. You're going to be a dad."* This surprise is ultimately not according to the plan, and their expectations must shift. There is vast uncertainty that the young couple must ride out as the events swirling around them increase in difficulty.

Great fear introduces itself in the event of an emergency c-section where there is the uncertainty of survival (before the late 1980s, preeclampsia often proved fatal to the mother, baby, or both). Even so, hope emerges as the anchor of their lives. How they hope is not unaware of the dire circumstances. However, it is all-knowing of them and still faithfully resolute in keeping hope.

References to the baby's name, "Ezekiel," and the father's reading of "a hopeless valley filled with dry bones" reflect a theme of hope in hopelessly impossible situations. Undergoing the peaks and valleys of progress and lack thereof tests the quality of the couple's hope. They experience both the challenge of their stamina (milk supply, attitude, support) and that of baby Ezekiel and his difficulties. Various medical procedures (inserting a P.I.C.C. line, an echocardiogram, a brain scan) appear as insurmountable "hurdles." They find each surmountable because of hope.

The respiratory therapist, "Mighty Joe," who performs CPR on Ezekiel, becomes a source of hope. He is hopeful precisely because of his hope's origin: "I just make a few changes here and there—this dial and that. . .and then God does the rest." This hope enables him to perform under the intensity of CPR on a preemie with greater focus and an undaunting determination. Hope is contagious, in a way, as it transmits and grows between individuals throughout the story.

The nature of the young couple's hope is in line with biblical hope, which sets the concepts of "hoping" and "waiting" in synonymous parallelism (Rom 8:24; 1 Cor 13:7). As difficult as it is, there is a strong sense of patience involved in biblical hope that is thematically present in their approach. The waiting seems tiresome, but the community of hope surrounding them (a father-in-law who parks the travel trailer in the parking lot, another NICU family striving in unison, encouraging nurses, and a perceptive doctor) fuels their confident expectation that what will be will be. Their hope is rooted in God but not dismissive of the reality of the circumstance and hardship of waiting.

In all their struggle, the family of three wind up overcoming through hope. While the outcome is not always happy (as with the family who previously lost a son at the same NICU), their own attitude and approach characterize hope as that which does not disappoint. At the story's close, the challenges remain. But hope has won the day.

Notes to Chapter 8

Chapter 8 focuses on expressing the biblical experience of *splagchnizomai*—often translated as "compassion"—using a story. This short story follows a formula of a linear pattern that switches between news reports and Cedric, the main character's, experience. *Splagchnizomai* means being moved in the inward parts—that is, in the heart, lungs, liver, and kidneys. This act of being physically moved in the bowels—from deep down—expresses compassion in such a way that one physically must move. The story's theme communicates how compassion entirely moves us to move.

The story's arc is of Cedric, a bowling alley manager, who becomes immersed in a tragic news story unfolding two thousand miles away. As he tries to accomplish simple, everyday tasks, his attention fixates on the Lees, a family of four missing in the snows of Oregon's wilderness. Throughout the eleven days, he becomes increasingly drawn into the family's plight and searches for ways to help. Cedric ultimately becomes so moved with compassion that he actually moves—he donates sacrificially, attempts to console by sending a letter, and sets out to join the search party.

This verb, *splagchnizomai*, shows up twelve times in the New Testament and is often used to express how Jesus is moved to heal or to lead.[1] *Splagchnizomai* is also used to express how the master felt as he forgave the soon-to-be unforgiving servant in Jesus's parable in Matthew 18:27. This all-consuming compassion is what the disgraced father felt when he saw his "prodigal son" return home in

1. Matt 9:36; 14:14; 15:32; 18:27; 20:34; Mark 1:41; 6:34; 8:2; 9:22; Luke 7:13; 10:33; 15:20.

Luke 15:20. He reacted as he ran to him, hugged him, kissed him, dressed him in a ring and robe, and prepared a feast for him. Jesus's parable in Luke 10 also describes a traveling Samaritan who comes across an injured man, sees him, is moved with compassion, and provides care to the injured man.

In the New Testament, *splagchnizomai* is always used in relation to Jesus—an action that Jesus experiences or a character in one of his parables. The characters in the parables experiencing *splagchnizomai* are each images representing God—the master of Matthew 18, the father in the "prodigal son" parable, and the "Good Samaritan" of Luke 10:25–37. In each episode, being moved with compassion manifests into physical movement. This short story images Cedric as filling these roles.

The story begins with the news of a family missing in the Oregon wilderness. Cedric is two thousand miles away, in the middle of his shift at the bowling alley. He is distracted and swept up by the breaking news story to the extent that he has trouble focusing at work. Although people go missing every day, this story, for some reason, grips Cedric with an all-consuming sense of compassion. The effect of *splagchnizomai* takes root inside him, producing an overwhelming urge to help this family in need.

For the next few days, Cedric is glued to the story. As he considers the Lee family's struggle for survival and rationing of food, he feels guilty reheating a chicken pot pie. Empathy for the grim experience of the family bleeds into his own.

Cedric rejoices when the news reveals that a helicopter pilot discovers Mrs. Lee and her daughters. However, with no word of Mr. Lee, Cedric's experience of *splagchnizomai* transforms to a new level. This *splagchnizomai* goes far beyond feeling sorry for their situation; it produces a gut-wrenching need to empathize and help. Since compassion was central to Jesus's self-understanding, it is the primary ethical virtue of the Christian life.[2] Therefore, following Jesus is to share in his large-heartedness and love that liberates all who suffer. For Cedric, this is an inescapable reality.

2. Marty, "Cultivating Compassion," 3.

Although Cedric and the Lees have no connection or relationship, Cedric cannot shake the urgency to support them. He tries writing letters and donating financially. His giving is sacrificial and to the point where it puts him in a financial overdraft. This act emphasizes the all-encompassing nature of *splagchnizomai*. His experience of *splagchnizomai* pushes him further to take off work, quit his job, if necessary, and join the search for Mr. Lee. Cedric's compassionate pursuit is contagious as his boss not only gives him the time off but also offers to contribute gas money. In the end, *splagchnizomai* rushes Cedric across three states to join the search, but the news comes over the radio waves that Mr. Lee's body was found. Regardless, Cedric has shown himself recklessly spendthrift in his pursuit of compassion. Cedric's actions parallel those of the Good Samaritan, the prodigal son's father, and the forgiving master of Matthew 18. Cedric embodies much of the reason people followed Jesus—they were drawn by his compassion as much as anything else. He possesses what Frederick Buechner describes as the "fatal capacity for feeling what it's like to live inside someone else's skin."[3]

3. Marty, "Cultivating Compassion," 3.

Notes to Chapter 9

THE BIBLICAL EXPERIENCE OF *aphiemi* is the focus of chapter 9. *Aphiemi* is typically translated "to forgive." However, it also bears the meaning "to send forth," "to send away," "to let go," or "to dispatch."[1] The storyline of chapter 9 sees the action *of aphiemi* as letting go, releasing, and sending away radically.

The formula for this short story is a linear narration reflecting on the past events of a family torn apart by strife. It moves into the present, where a young girl grapples with the reality of *aphiemi* and the opportunity to forgive in a radical way her undeserving father. Chapter 9's story arc involves an alcoholic and abusive father who abandons his wife and two children. The daughter, Sophia, as a result, is marred by insecurity, bitterness, and rage. As she struggles through the tragic newness, her crumbling world is interrupted by *aphiemi*. The concept of *aphiemi* guides her toward radical forgiveness and "letting go," not only for her father's sake but much for her own.

Chapter 9 opens with Sophia reflecting on recent events that have upturned her life and home. She stands resolute in her inability to forgive. The scene is the aftermath of domestic violence, emotional abuse, and the destruction of physical property. Sophia's father and mother have had another fight in the living room, but this time her father has resolved to cut ties with the family and go. To make matters worse, Sophia's father ransacks the apartment, even taking the coins from the children's piggybanks before he goes. This betrayal is unthinkable for a father and further seeps hurt and brokenness into Sophia's relationship with him. The chronic

1. Bailes, "On the Physical Death," 2752.

violence finally leads to abandonment and leaves Sophia in a place of emptiness and disbelief.

After her father departs from the family, Sophia cannot quite grip the new reality. She waits by the window for his return and listens for a knock at the door. Her imagination paints a false, rosy picture of her father returning as a changed man who looks and acts nothing like the one who left. She pictures her father's transformation, a moment of forgiveness, and the process toward reconciliation. However, it is merely an imagination.

Instead, this new reality of her father's abandonment has Sophia drowning in despair, falling behind in school, wrestling with identity, self-worth, and a sprouting bitterness. Although the apartment is set back to its normal state, the marks of abuse remain on her mother's body. The emotional toll has created deep gashes in the family emotionally and financially. Without any luck, Sophia continues searching for her father on the bus, out the window, and placing phone calls. All the conditions allow Sophia's bitterness and hatred for her father to take root. Naturally, she experiences the effects of abandonment and isolation.

However, Sophia meets Marsha Simmons, an ailing shut-in from chapter 5, in the mailroom of their apartment building. Toting along her oxygen tank, Ms. Simmons stops Sophia to provide an opportunity for Sophia to talk about the ongoing situation crippling her family. Ms. Simmons knows the circumstances because she lives in the apartment directly below Sophia. She attempts to become an ally or support for Sophia by providing a safe place to talk or visit. Unfortunately, Sophia is tightlipped and unwilling to divulge the details of her pain because it feels like a betrayal.

Ms. Simmons sees how the perpetual violence and abuse have warped Sophia's perspective. So, she goes about reaching Sophia by another route. As she delivers a plate of peanut butter cookies, Ms. Simmons also gives Sophia an old National Geographic with a doge-ared article, "Astonishing Stories From Rwanda." For the next hour and a half, Sophia consumes the cookies and takes her mind off the struggle of loss and abandonment. When she reaches the stories of radical forgiveness from Rwanda, Sophia reads about Jean Ngenzi, whose entire family is murdered in the Hutu genocide of 1994.

Jean undergoes trauma counseling, moves through his rage and determination to kill specific Hutu perpetrators, and takes steps toward forgiveness. "I learned it's not 'forgive and forget,'" Jean says, as he expresses how forgiving means remembering and making the conscious decision to operate differently. This aspect of *aphiemi* sees forgiveness as removing a substance in the act of "sending away" the wrongdoing and relieving debt in "letting go."[2] However, Jean also details the reality that justice still goes hand in hand with forgiveness. His work now as a Child Protection Officer in Rwanda proves his drive toward radical forgiveness as he hires Hutus and has even married one.

The second story from Rwanda that Sophia reads is about Colette Gasana. Colette also witnessed her family's murder and the handicapping of her grandmother at the hands of her Hutu neighbors. For Colette, a Christian program has helped her in the process of forgiveness. Her experience with forgiveness has become so radical that she created an organization called "Rwanda Kids" that seeks to care for Tutsi and Hutu orphans. Her attitude of *aphiemi* is apparent in her statement, "I learned Love." The verb *aphiemi* highlights how forgiveness is, like love, not a feeling but an action involving the will rather than emotions.[3] By sponsoring the son of the incarcerated man who murdered Colette's parents, Colette is actively living out the love of radical forgiveness. She is living out forgiveness, based upon her involvement with a Christian program, in a manner that realizes how forgiveness of sins is the result of faith in Jesus.[4] Therefore, how forgiveness becomes a part of one's experience should mirror the active forgiveness of Jesus.[5]

The stories of Jean and Colette embody the forgiveness of Jesus. The forgiveness of wrongs is central to Jesus's ethical teachings.[6]

2. Roitto, "Polyvalence of ἀφίημι," 144.

3. Mackey, "Forgiveness Isn't Something," 2.

4. Killgallen, "Faith and Forgiveness," 225

5. Matt 6:14–15; 18:21–22; Mark 11:25; Eph 1:7–8; Col 1:13–14; 1 John 1:9.

6. Matt 18:21–22.

Equally so is the emphasis on forgiving others when they sin against you. This way, "Your Heavenly Father will also forgive you."[7]

As her tears fall on Ms. Simmons's magazine and during her follow-up conversation with Ms. Simmons, Sophia is coming to terms with the complex reality of *aphiemi*. Aphiemi is not some burden that is too great to bear, but it is the release of a burden that she already bears.[8] Therefore, the story closes with Sophia mulling over a final thought about the deservingness and prompting of forgiveness. Also present is the emergence of Ms. Simmons as one who counsels the vulnerable and becomes a protector, all while sharing the complexity of her own first-hand forgiveness experience.

7. Matt 6:14.

8. Mackey, "Forgiveness Isn't Something," 3.

Notes to Chapter 10

Chapter 10 focuses on expressing the biblical experience of *sha-lom*—often translated as "peace"—using a story. A dialogue interchange dominates this short story. It follows a linear pattern toward a direction of completion or wholeness.

Shalom is a wide-ranging term in the Old Testament, referring to wholeness, abundant life, well-being, completeness, satisfactory conditions, soundness, peace, and salvation.[1] *Shalom* is too big a word for anything in the English language as it describes how the world ought to be. The vast diversity of the word produces the vision of an integrated wholeness of relationships and a state of mind that is at peace and satisfied where nothing is lacking.[2] This short story focuses on several the nuances of *shalom*, with particular attention to *shalom* as proper functioning and wholeness.

The story's arc is of three men who spend an afternoon in a barn restoring a tractor to function properly. Fixing the tractor (producing *shalom*—wholeness/proper functioning) parallels the restoration of Jimmy, one of the three men in the barn. The image of *shalom* presented in this story attempts to encapsulate a diversity of meaning—from a physical state of well-being to things being as they ought to be in the material world.[3]

The story opens with Mike, the hardware store owner (mentioned in chapters 1, 2, and 4), picking up Jimmy and driving to Uncle Charlie's to help the older man fix his broken-down tractor.

1. Franklin, "Searching for Shalom," 3.

2. Franklin, "Searching for Shalom," 3.

3. Yoder, *Shalom*, 13.

On the way to Uncle Charlie's, Jimmy and Mike talk about the struggles that Jimmy experiences as a young father trying to manage the pressures of marriage, parenting, work, and home life. Jimmy continues reiterating the phrase "Goes with the territory" to suggest that things are the way they are, and that's that. This state of things going "with the territory" reflect an apathy toward the incompleteness and un-wholeness of a world void of peace. Peacelessness is the status quo unless peace is intentionally introduced into the situation. Therefore, Jimmy's life thematically represents the breakdown or absence of *shalom*. He is experiencing the doldrums of life in such a way that he feels something is missing or not functioning properly.

In the history of Israel, during the tribal confederacy and in the monarchy, *shalom* broke down. In a real sense, the vision of *shalom* failed to be realized.[4] The prophet Jeremiah weeps over Judah's situation and denounces the false prophets, "They have healed the wound of my people lightly, saying *Shalom, Shalom* when there is no *Shalom*."[5] Comparatively, Jimmy's life shows signs of a *shalom* breakdown. He's apathetic about the situation and complains about the grinding nature of his circumstances. Fortunately, in the life of Israel (and thematically in Jimmy's), the stage is set for Jeremiah's prophecy of a new covenant of *shalom*.[6] This form of eschatological *shalom* is also expressed in Isaiah's "Prince of Peace" (Isa 9), Ezekiel's covenant of peace (Ezek 34, 37), and Second Isaiah's "Suffering Servant" (Isa 53).

The Old Testament records peace offerings in connection with the expression of thanksgiving (Lev 7:12, 13, 15; 2 Chron 30:22; 31:2; 33:16), and this interchange points toward the union of peace with thanks. Mike, introduced in chapter 2 as Paul's Alcoholics Anonymous sponsor, functions as a bringer of this eschatological *shalom*. As he breaks out techniques from the A.A. program, Mike helps Jimmy to identify areas where he can recognize gratitude and gratefulness.

Inside Uncle Charlie's barn, the three men assess the issues preventing the tractor from experiencing *shalom* (proper functioning)

4. Watlner, "Shalom and Wholeness," 146.

5. Jer 6:14.

6. Jer 31.

and simultaneously assess Jimmy's situation. *Shalom,* in this scene, expands into a communal ordeal of creating wholeness. The wholeness of an individual can never be realized apart from wholeness in the community, thus linking individual and communal wholeness.[7] The men seek to produce shalom in this authentic and nurturing community. The small community (Mike and Uncle Charlie) addresses Jimmy's situation by pinpointing what seems to be preventing peace (dissatisfaction, irritation, disillusionment, lack of purpose and vision, giving "leftovers" instead of focused attention). Meanwhile, Mike is evaluating and fixing the issue preventing the tractor from properly functioning.

The paralleling stories come together when Jimmy finally sits on the pan seat to test the rebuilt carburetor. This moment with the peaceless Jimmy atop a malfunctioning tractor is the comparative image of creating wholeness in an environment lacking *shalom.* After a misfire, Jimmy manages to start up the tractor. As he looks down from behind the wheel and beams, he shouts his persistent phrase, "Goes with the territory!" as if to say that this is the way things go. However, the scene closes with Mike's correction, "The hell it does, Jimmy! We rebuilt the territory!" Mike's point is that the tractor functions properly because the changes and conditions were established to make it so. The impetus is that if Jimmy were to make the proper changes and alterations, perhaps *shalom* could also be achieved and experienced in his situation. On the ride home, Jimmy reflects on the experience and how he "feels more taken apart and put back together in the process." As something profound in the depth of his everything has shifted, Jimmy is left with a decision to make. He can either live into *shalom* as proper functioning and wholeness or continue going "with the territory."

7. Watlner, "Shalom and Wholeness," 146.

Bibliography

Bailes, G. S. "On the Physical Death of Jesus Christ." *JAMA* (1986) 2752.

Bloom, Maureen. "The Legacy of 'Sacred' and 'Profane' in Ancient Israel: Interpretations of Durkheim's Classifications." *Jewish Studies Quarterly* 5 (1998) 103–23.

Bonhoeffer, Dietrich. *Letters and Papers from Prison*. Edited by Eberhard Bethge. New York: Macmillan, 1953.

Bovon, François, and Christine M. Thomas. *Luke 1: A Commentary on the Gospel of Luke 1:1—9:50*. Edited by Helmut Koester. Minneapolis: 1517 Media, 2002.

Brown, Driver, and Briggs. *A Hebrew and English Lexicon of the Old Testament*. Oxford: Clarendon, 1962.

Brueggemann, Walter. *An Introduction to the Old Testament: The Canon and Christian Imagination*. Louisville: Westminster John Knox, 2003.

Bultmann, Rudolf. "Elpis." In *Theological Dictionary of the New Testament*, edited by Gerhard Kittel, et al., 3:517. Grand Rapids: Eerdmans, 1962.

Danker, Frederick, et al. *A Greek-English Lexicon of the New Testament and Other Early Christian Literature*. Chicago: University of Chicago Press, 2000.

Denton, David R. "Hope and Perseverance." *Scottish Journal of Theology* 34 (1981) 313–20.

Drance, Georgel. "Holy." *Ecumenica* 7 (2014) 21–23.

Eichrodt, Walther. *Theology of the Old Testament*. Vol. 1. Philadelphia: Westminster, 1961.

Fox, Michael. "Ṭôb as Covenant Terminology." *Bulletin of the American Schools of Oriental Research* 209 (1973) 41–42.

Franklin, Kirk J. "Searching for Shalom: Transformation in the Mission of God and the Bible Translation Movement." *HTS Theological Studies* 76 (2020) 1–10.

Fredriksen, Paula. "Paul's Letter to the Romans, the Ten Commandments, and Pagan 'Justification by Faith.'" *Journal of Biblical Literature* 133 (2014) 801–8.

Griswold, Charles L., and David Konstan. *Ancient Forgiveness*. Cambridge: Cambridge University Press, 2012.

Haugen, Gary. "Gary Haugen: Joy Is the Oxygen." Interview by Kate Bowler. Everything Happens (podcast), May 2020. http://www.katebowler.com/podcasts/gary-haugen-joy-is-the-oxygen/.

Hay, David M. "*Pistis* as 'Ground for Faith' in Hellenized Judaism and Paul." *Journal of Biblical Literature* 108 (1989) 461–76.

Hays, Richard B. *The Faith of Jesus Christ: An Investigation of the Narrative Substructure of Galatians 3:1—4:11*. Society of Biblical Literature Dissertation Series 56. Chico: Scholars, 1983.

Hemingway, Ernest. *The Old Man and the Sea*. New York: Scribner Paperback Fiction, 1995.

Hollinshead, Jay K. "'What Is Good for Man?': An Exposition of Ecclesiastes 7:1–14." *Bibliotheca Sacra* 170 (2013) 31–50.

Inselmann, Anke. "Emotions and Passions in the New Testament: Methodological Issues." *Biblical Interpretation* 24 (2016) 536–54.

Jenni, Ernst, and Claus Westermann. *Theological Lexicon of the Old Testament*. Vol. 2. Translated by Mark E. Biddle. Peabody, MA: Hendrickson, 1997.

Kilgallen, J. J. "Faith and Forgiveness: Luke VII, 36–50." *Revue Biblique* 108 (2001) 214–27.

Kim, Sung-Jin, and Nga Thi Hong Hoang. "An Analysis of the Literary Allusion in Ecclesiastes 2 to the Creation Narrative in Genesis 1–2: Rhetorical Role of the Creation Motif in Ecclesiastes 2." *ACTS 신학저널* 41 (2019) 9–40.

Lienhard, Joseph T., ed. *Exodus, Leviticus, Numbers, Deuteronomy*. Downers Grove, IL: InterVarsity, 2001.

Mackey, Geoffrey. "Forgiveness Isn't Something You Feel. It's Something You Do (Especially When It's Hard)." *America* 3 (2021) 1–3.

Marty, Peter W. "Cultivating Compassion." *Christian Century* 139 (2022) 3.

Minear, P. S. "Hope." In *The Interpreters Dictionary of the Bible*, edited by George Arthur Buttrick, 2:641. Nashville: Abingdon, 1962.

Morgan, Teresa. *Roman Faith and Christian Faith: Pistis and Fides in the Early Roman Empire and Early Churches*. Oxford: Oxford University Press, 2015.

Morin, Scott, and Mandy Nelson. "Tov: An Explosive Word." *And Sons Magazine*, 2021. https://www.andsonsmagazine.com/inspiration/tov-an-explosive-word.

Myers, B. L. *Walking with the Poor: Principles and Practices of Transformational Development*. Maryknoll, NY: Orbis, 1999.

O'Rourke, John J. "'Pistis' in Romans." *Catholic Biblical Quarterly* 35 (1973) 88–94.

Otto, Rudolph. *The Idea of the Holy: An Inquiry into the Non-Rational Factor in the Idea of the Divine and its Relation to the Rational*. New York: Oxford University Press, 1958.

Owiredu, Charles. "Sin Is a Person: Some Ontological Metaphors in the Bible." *Acta Theologica* 41 (2021) 87–100.

Proctor, Mark A. "'Who Is My Neighbor?' Recontextualizing Luke's Good Samaritan (Luke 10:25–37)." *Journal of Biblical Literature* 138 (2019) 203–19.

Renard, John. *Crossing Confessional Boundaries: Exemplary Lives in Jewish, Christian, and Islamic Traditions.* Oakland: University of California Press, 2020.

Richert, Virginia Gerbrandt. "Faith Formation for Leaders Today." *Canadian Mennonite* (2016) 16.

Rogers, Patrick. "Hopeful, in Spite of Chains: The Indomitable Spirit of Paul, in the Captivity Letters." *Biblical Theology Bulletin* 12 (1982) 77–81.

Roitto, Rikard. "The Polyvalence of ἀφίημι and the Two Cognitive Frames of Forgiveness in the Synoptic Gospels." *Novum Testamentum* 57 (2015) 136–58.

Silker, Jeffrey. *Sin in the New Testament.* New York: Oxford University Press, 2020.

Sloyan, Gerard S. "The Joy of Christ." *Furrow* 11 (1960) 91–98.

Ukeachusim, Chidinma Precious, et al. "Understanding Compassion in the Gospel of Matthew (Matthew 14:13–21)." *Theology Today* 77 (2021) 372–92.

Van Rensburg, J. J. J. "The Children of God in Romans 8." *Neotestamentica* 15 (1981) 139–76.

Volf, Miroslav. *Free of Charge: Giving and Forgiving in a Culture Stripped of Grace.* Grand Rapids: Zondervan, 2005.

Waltner, Erland. "Shalom and Wholeness." *Brethren Life and Thought* 29 (1984) 145–51.

Waters, Sonia. "Getting More Than You Paid For: The Parable of the Treasure and the Pearl as the Experience of Transformation." *Pastoral Psychology* 61 (2012) 423–34.

Whitley, C. F. "The Semantic Range of Ḥesed." *Biblica* 62 (1981) 519–26.

Winger, Michael. "From Grace to Sin: Names and Abstractions in Paul's Letters." *Novum Testamentum* 41 (1999) 145–75.

Yoder, P. B. *Shalom: The Bible's Word for Salvation, Justice, & Peace.* Eugene, OR: Wipf & Stock, 1997.

Ziegert, Carsten. "What Is חֶסֶד?: A Frame-Semantic Approach." *Journal for the Study of the Old Testament* 44 (2020) 711–32.

Zimmerli, Walther, et al. *Ezekiel 1: A Commentary on the Book of the Prophet Ezekiel, Chapters 1–24.* Minneapolis: Augsburg Fortress, 1979.